Under water Dig

The Excavation of a Revolutionary War Privateer

BY BARBARA FORD

Alligators, Raccoons, and Other Survivors
The Wildlife of the Future

Why Does a Turtle Live Longer Than a Dog?
A Report on Animal Longevity

BY BARBARA FORD AND RONALD R. KEIPER

The Island Ponies
An Environmental Study of Their Life on Assateague

Under water Dig

The Excavation of a Revolutionary War Privateer

by Barbara Ford and David C. Switzer

illustrated with photographs

William Morrow and Company   New York   1982

C.2

Printed in the United States of America.
1   2   3   4   5   6   7   8   9   10

Library of Congress Cataloging in Publication Data

Ford, Barbara.
   Underwater dig.

   Includes index.
   Summary: An account of the exploration of a shipwreck in Penobscot Bay, Maine, highlights the new science of nautical archaeology and illuminates a disastrous, overlooked defeat in American naval history.
   1. Penobscot Expedition, 1779—Juvenile literature.   2. Defence (Ship : Mass.)—Juvenile literature.   3. Underwater archaeology—Juvenile literature.   [1. Penobscot Expedition, 1779.   2. Defence (Ship : Mass.)   3. Underwater archaeology]   I. Switzer, David C.   II. Title.
   E235.F68   1982   973.3'5   82-6440
   ISBN 0-688-01475-5

Photo Credits

American Institute of Nautical Archeology, pp. 102, (Roger Smith, photographer) 35, 84, 86, 91, 107; Barbara Ford, pp. 19, 23, 28, 31, 49, 50, 65, 69, 89, 99, 101, 111, 120-122, 124, 127, 129, 141; Peter Hentschel, pp. 43 (bottom), 83 (bottom), 100, 130-131, 132-133, 139, 142; MIT Sea Grant College Program, pp. 36, 56-57; Maine State Museum, pp. 55, 67, 68 (bottom), 70, 72 (both), 74, 76, 80, 82, 87, 88, 92, 117, 136, 140, 144-145; The Mariners Museum, Newport News, Virginia, p. 14; Museum of Fine Arts, Boston, Gift of Joseph W., William B., and Edward H.R. Revere, p. 17; National Maritime Museum, Greenwich, England, p. 22; Cynthia Orr, p. 104 (top); David B. Price, p. 146; William F. Searle, pp. 34, 38, 43 (top), 44, 45; Diane E. Smith, p. 39; Sheli Smith, p. 21; David C. Switzer, pp. 52 (bottom), 53, 60, 61, 64, 68 (top), 71, 109, 116, 123, 125; Carol Voss, p. 104 (bottom); Philip Voss, p. 52 (top), 63, 83 (top), 96, 106, 137; David Wyman, pp. 112-113. Permission is gratefully acknowledged.

Contents

Under water Dig

The Excavation of a Revolutionary War Privateer

Foreword

In 1972, a group of professors and students from the Massachusetts Institute of Technology and Maine Maritime Academy discovered a shipwreck in an inlet on the coast of Maine in Penobscot Bay. Artifacts and historical research identified the wreck as the remains of a privateer that sank during the American Revolution. Beginning in 1975 and continuing for six years during the summer months, the wreck has been the object of a nautical archeological project devoted to retrieving artifacts and from them learning more about ships and the seamen who served on them during the Colonial era. Here is the story of that project, beginning with an episode from the Revolutionary War that took place in 1779.

1

The Penobscot Expedition

On July 19, 1779, the largest military and naval expedi‚ tion ever mounted by the Americans during the Revolutionary War set sail from Boston, Massachusetts. After picking up reinforcements at Townsend, a seaport north of Boston, it headed for Penobscot Bay, 170 miles to the northeast. (Penobscot Bay was then part of Massachusetts, but today it is located in Maine.)

A few weeks earlier, word had reached Boston that a British force had occupied Bagaduce, a small town on a peninsula in Penobscot Bay. It consisted of about 700 soldiers and three warships, the report said, and a fort was being erected to guard the harbor from attack.

For the Americans, British troops at Bagaduce were a major threat. The town occupied a very strategic location because of its position near the mouth of the Penobscot River. From Bagaduce, the British would have been able to control the river and take steps to establish a new colony that would be loyal to the crown. A name had already been chosen for the colony: New Ireland. The goal of the expedition that left Boston in July of 1779 was to force the enemy to withdraw from the area.

The *Diligent*, the brig on the left,
was one of the American ships in the Penobscot Expedition.
She flies the British colors in this painting, which shows her
being captured by an American ship earlier in the Revolutionary
War.

To carry out this mission, a fleet of forty-three vessels had been assembled, nineteen of which were armed. The Continental Navy contributed three warships, one a brand-new thirty-three-gun frigate, the *Warren*. It was the flagship of the expedition commander. Massachusetts contributed another three warships from her state navy. There were thirteen more vessels called privateers. Privateers were privately owned vessels that were authorized by the Government to capture enemy shipping. The officers and crewmen of privateers received shares of the profits earned through the sale of the captured vessel and its cargo.

Because privateering was such a lucrative business, many shipowners converted their vessels to privateers and others built ships solely for privateering. One of the ships that joined the fleet at Townsend in July of 1779 had been built specifically as a privateer, probably at Beverly, Massachusetts. Her name was *Defence*, and she had been launched very recently. In fact, she may have been on her first voyage. The *Defence* carried sixteen cannon capable of firing six-pound balls. She was classed as a brig because of her two masts and her square sails. The masts were over seventy feet high; her deck was eighty to ninety feet long.

About 100 men were aboard the *Defence*, far more than were needed to sail her. The extra crew members would man the guns, board enemy ships, and carry out other activities connected with the expedition. The captain was John Edmonds, who may have come from Beverly too.

The rest of the expedition was made up of unarmed sloops and schooners, one- and two-masted vessels that were used as troop transports and supply ships. In all, the expedition carried about 2,000 men.

The man who had been selected to command the Penobscot Expedition was Dudley Saltonstall, a captain in the Continental Navy. General Solomon Lovell was given the command of the land forces. The most famous name among the expedition leaders was Paul Revere, the same Paul Revere who had made the immortal "midnight ride" four years earlier. Revere was in charge of the ordinance or field artillery, the cannon that would be used against the British fortifications. Neither Commodore Saltonstall nor the other leaders had much military experience.

Still, the odds seemed to be in favor of the American fleet as it sailed toward Penobscot Bay. It had three times as many men as were in the British force, as well as more ships and guns. The three British warships at Penobscot Bay had a total of only 56 cannon, compared to the 350 carried aboard the American vessels. But the Americans had liabilities that were not as apparent as their advantages. Not only did the American officers lack experience; so did the men. Most of them were poorly trained militiamen. The only professional soldiers among the Americans was a detachment of marines.

The British, on the other hand, were veterans of many battles. They also had an advantage which neither they nor the Americans knew about as yet. About the time the American fleet left Boston, word of the Penobscot Expe-

Paul Revere was one of the American leaders
of the Penobscot Expedition.

dition reached New York City, which was held by the British during most of the Revolution. Shortly after the American fleet reached Penobscot, a British fleet was on its way north from New York to help its comrades. The British fleet, under the command of Sir George Collier, was much stronger. Although it too had only six warships, the largest, the *Raisonnable,* carried sixty-four guns—twice as many as did the *Warren*—and was much more solidly built. The fleet also had two thirty-two-gun ships.

The American fleet took five days to reach Penobscot Bay, a long, wide body of water with many inlets and islands. On July 25, the half-completed Fort George on the heights of Bagaduce Peninsula came into sight. The British ships were anchored off the peninsula. Neither side wasted any time. As commands of "Fire!" rang out, cannons barked from the ships, from Fort George, and from Nautilus Island just to the east of Bagaduce, where the British had a gun emplacement. The firing continued for about two hours, but little damage was done on either side.

That evening the Americans, supported by fire from the *Defence* and two other ships, took Nautilus Island. Paul Revere directed the emplacement of the cannon, so fire could be directed toward the fort and the British vessels.

Early on July 28, the Americans made a landing on the peninsula and quickly fought their way up the wooded slopes to a point just 600 feet from Fort George. Although they had suffered heavy losses, military experts agree

Fort George today.

that they could have taken the fort at this point. When General Lovell arrived, however, he gave the order to dig in. It was the Americans' first big mistake.

As the commodore in command of the fleet, Saltonstall was supposed to support the landing with fire from his ships and then attack the three British warships anchored off Bagaduce. He fulfilled the first part of his role, but after Lovell's troops dug in the American fleet did no more than sail back and forth some distance from the British warships. Occasionally an American ship fired a cannonball at the enemy. Over the next two weeks, Lovell tried to persuade Saltonstall to attack the British fleet in support of a land attack on the fort. The commodore always found a reason not to cooperate.

Morale among the Americans in front of Fort George crumbled as their officers wrangled. Many soldiers deserted by walking over the lightly guarded neck of land that connected the peninsula to the mainland. The rest seemed to have lost the will to fight. There were several small skirmishes between the Americans and the British, which the British won easily, even though they had fewer men. During this tense period, Paul Revere irritated both officers and men by having himself rowed back to his ship several times a day for hot meals.

A few days after the Americans had landed on Bagaduce, Saltonstall received a letter carried by a messenger ship. It was from the Continental Navy Board and enclosed a sworn legal statement from a man who claimed the British relief squadron would soon sail from New York to aid Fort George. The letter, however, seems to have had no more effect on Saltonstall than Lovell's pleas for naval support. Only when Saltonstall received a later message from the Navy Board, this one ordering him to attack the British ships off Bagaduce, did he agree to act. The same mail brought more bad news. A British squadron was definitely on its way to Penobscot Bay to help Fort George.

The long-awaited land and sea attack by the Americans was finally scheduled to begin on the foggy afternoon of August 13, three weeks after they had arrived. Lovell's troops prepared for the final assault on Fort George while Saltonstall's fleet sailed toward the

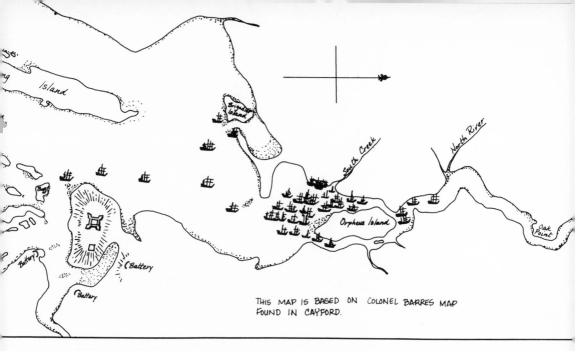

THIS MAP IS BASED ON COLONEL BARRES MAP FOUND IN CAYFORD.

This copy of an historical map shows the American fleet
fleeing the British. The *Defence* is probably the ship at the top,
nearest Brigadier's Island. Most of the fleet is heading
up the Penobscot River to the right.

British ships off Bagaduce. Just as the two sides were
about to close, Saltonstall received word that a lookout
ship had spotted sails coming up the Bay. They belonged
to the British fleet from New York. The American attack
was promptly called off, and the order to retreat given.

By dawn of August 14, the American troops on Bagaduce had been evacuated, along with all the cannon they
had taken with them. The *Defence* may have participated
in the evacuation.

But more trouble was in store for the Americans. The
British fleet, now joined by the three ships that had been
defending Bagaduce, lay between the American fleet and
the open sea. If the American warships had engaged in
battle with the British at this point, some of the other

21

The British fleet sailing up Penobscot Bay.

ships might have escaped the trap. Saltonstall, however, chose to run. There were only two escape routes: down the extreme western side of the Bay or up the Penobscot River at the head of the Bay. The river's mouth was about seven miles from Bagaduce.

Most of the fleet headed toward the river, but the *Defence,* the *Hunter,* and the *Hampden* decided to sail west. The *Hunter,* overloaded with guns and men, was soon cut off and captured after she ran aground. The *Hampden* was also captured. They were the only American ships actually taken by the British.

The other American ships reached the Penobscot River, but the British were close behind. Dudley Saltonstall, aboard the *Warren,* abandoned his unarmed

22

troopships and headed upstream. Some of the faster ships got as far as twenty miles upstream until a waterfall stopped them. The rest were scattered along the lower reaches of the Penobscot. Realizing there was no escaping their pursuers, the American captains ran their vessels aground one by one and set them afire to keep them out of the hands of the British. The sound of explosions filled the night as fire reached each ship's magazine, where ammunition was stored.

Early the next morning the crew of the HMS *Blonde* caught up with the *Warren*, which had gone only two miles upstream. Suddenly the American ship exploded.

The *Defence* was one of the last American ships on the Penobscot Expedition to remain afloat and in American hands. She had sailed west, like the *Hunter* and the *Hampden*, but instead of continuing down the coast of the Bay she entered Stockton Harbor, an inlet west of the

The *Defence* entered Stockton Harbor,
an inlet west of the Penobscot River.

Penobscot River. Captain Edmonds' plan of escape is hard to determine; perhaps he hoped to be able to sail over a bar between Brigadier's Island and the mainland on the rising tide. Then he might have been able to proceed down the western shore of the Bay after dark without being seen. A local pilot was aboard, and he may have suggested this tactic.

If so, it didn't work. When the *Defence* entered Stockton Harbor, she was spotted by the British ship HMS *Camilla* under a Captain Collins. The *Camilla* anchored near the harbor mouth. Captain Collins made this entry in his log:

> Anchored at 9:00 . . . in 10 fathoms. Sent the boat manned and armed to destroy a RebelBrigg . . . at half past 11:00 Boat returned, at 2:00 AM heard the explosion of the said Brigg.

On August 20, Commodore Sir George Collier described the end of the *Defence* in a letter to the British Admiralty.

> I directed Capt. Collins of the *Camilla* to proceed into the inlet and take or destroy the *Defence*. That measure was not carried into Effect, by her blowing herself up . . . She was a new Brig carrying 16 six pounders.

As far as is known, all the men aboard the *Defence* survived. Captain Edmonds took command of another

Massachusetts privateer, also called the *Defence*, before the Revolution ended in 1783. A total of about 500 Americans died on the Penobscot Expedition, but the rest escaped from the burning ships and eventually made their way back to Boston. Saltonstall, Lovell, and Revere were among the survivors. All faced court-martial and public inquiry when they returned. Revere was censured at the court-martial, but he was cleared of blame in 1782. Lovell was cleared from the beginning.

The man on whom most of the blame for the failure of the Penobscot Expedition fell was Dudley Saltonstall. He was dismissed from the Continental Navy and finished the war serving as a privateer captain.

There is still controversy among historians over the roles played by the leaders of the Penobscot Expedition, but all agree on one point. It was the worst naval defeat in American history.

2

The
Defence
Is Found

For over 200 years, the remains of the ships sunk after the Penobscot Expedition disaster have lain beneath the waters of the Penobscot River. Some of their iron and bronze cannon have been raised from time to time. In the 1950's, workmen digging holes for a new bridge at Bangor came across several cannon in the river. The guns were identified as having come from vessels of the Penobscot fleet. One cannon can be seen today in a park near the end of the bridge.

The only ship ever found in the river was the *Warren*, the flagship from which Commodore Dudley Saltonstall directed the American attempt to capture Bagaduce. Its remains—part of a charred hull—are visible at low tide near the town of Winterport. But the rest of the Penobscot fleet seemed to have vanished forever.

In 1963, Dean Mayhew joined the faculty of Maine Maritime Academy in Castine as a professor of history. Castine is what Bagaduce, the site of Fort George, is known as today. Only one house in the town still stands from the period of the Penobscot Expedition. The fort has become a park. Maine Maritime Academy trains officers for the ships that make up our Merchant Marine. The campus is just below the site of Fort George.

Professor Mayhew had been interested in the Penobscot Expedition since he was a student, and when he

The buildings of the Maine Maritime Academy lie below Fort George.

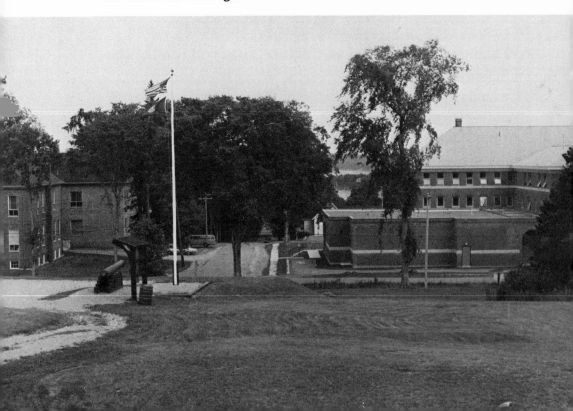

found himself near the site of the battle, he began to research it more thoroughly. He read old books, checked the records of the British Admiralty, and talked to local townspeople. Before long, he became convinced that the wreck of one ship, the *Defence*, was located in Stockton Harbor. Sears Island, known as Brigadier's Island during the days of the Revolution, forms one shore of the harbor.

Mayhew's belief rested on three clues. In a letter sent to the British Admiralty by Sir George Collier after the American defeat, the British admiral stated that an enemy vessel had been caught in Stockton Harbor. Her name was *Defence*. A second clue came from Cappy Hall, a fisherman who lived near Stockton. He told Mayhew that he had once snagged his nets on something in Stockton Harbor near Sears Island. The third clue was in the papers of a local historian, who reported cannons being found off Sears Island.

Mayhew discussed his findings with colleagues at the Academy but failed to arouse much interest. Some students took small boats over to the harbor and poked around on the muddy bottom without any results. What was needed, Mayhew realized, was sophisticated electronic equipment to search the murky waters of the harbor and divers to check out the findings. But there were no funds to carry out such a project. So there the matter rested for almost ten years.

In 1972, the Maine Maritime Academy organized a summer workshop in ocean engineering for students from the Academy and the Massachusetts Institute of Technology (MIT) in Cambridge, Massachusetts. The

United States Department of Commerce sponsored the workshop through its Sea Grant program. One of the workshop projects was to teach students how to build and operate a sonar device.

Originally sonar had been used during World War II to detect submarines by means of sound waves. After the war, sonar was converted to other underwater work, thanks to the efforts of MIT professor Dr. Harold Edgerton. Early sonar indicated the presence of an underwater object by returning sonar echos, or beeps. The faster the beeps, the closer the object. Today sonar records its findings on a strip of paper and makes a picture or shadow of the object.

When the sonar project was being discussed, someone remarked that what was really needed was a target, something to search for on the bottom of Penobscot Bay.

"What about the wreck in Stockton Harbor?" asked one of the Academy teachers, remembering Mayhew's research.

Mayhew brought in the chart on which Cappy Hall had marked the location of the object that had snagged his net. After looking at the chart and hearing Mayhew's evidence that a wreck might possibly be in Stockton Harbor, the workshop faculty agreed that it would make a fine target for the sonar project.

That summer the workshop students built a sonar unit that included a bullet-shaped "fish" to be towed behind a boat. They also redesigned a depth recorder to be placed in the boat. When the sonar was in operation, the fish would give off underwater sound waves that would appear on the depth recorder. The whole apparatus was very simple.

When the boat with the sonar on board left Castine early one July morning, three members of the ocean engineering workshop faculty and four student divers were aboard. Captain William F. Searle, the director of the workshop, and Herman Kunz were both retired United States Navy salvage experts. David Wyman was a professor of ocean engineering and naval architecture at the Maine Maritime Academy. One of his jobs was to serve as skipper of the boat.

The trip to Stockton Harbor from Castine takes about an hour by small boat. The harbor is a quiet area even today, with few buildings near the shore. Although people lived on Sears Island during the Revolution and afterward, it is uninhabited today.

In the harbor, the boat surveyed one small area at a time, moving slowly back and forth like a person mow-

Sears Island, known as Brigadier's Island
during the Revolutionary War, forms one shore of Stockton Harbor.

ing a lawn. Two days passed. The survey team saw no features on the strip of paper attached to the recorder. The seabed seemed absolutely flat. Then, on the third day, David Wyman was watching the sonar unit when he saw a dark spot with shadows behind it appear on the recorder. This kind of mark means something is sticking up above the seabed. As the boat cruised slowly along, two more marks appeared. All three were very close together.

The boat anchored in the middle of the cluster of marks, about 200 yards from Sears Island in twenty-five feet of water. The student divers put on wet suits and scuba gear and jumped into the water. Almost immediately the head of one diver popped back up above the surface. Taking his breathing regulator out of his mouth, he shouted, "There's a cannon down here!"

As it turned out, the diver didn't actually see a cannon. What he saw and felt was a large irregular mass of metal half buried in the mud of the bottom. Iron and certain other metals undergo chemical changes in salt water that result in the formation of a concretion. A concretion is made up of deteriorating metal, marine organisms, and other material that sticks to the metal. The Stockton Harbor concretion might have been a cannon, but it might also have been something else.

The divers took down a tape measure and carefully measured the concretion. It was about seven feet long and two feet wide, easily big enough for a cannon.

Not long after the first cannon-sized object had been discovered, another was found nearby. In the same area was a square brick structure with mortar still holding most of the bricks together. Pieces of wood were scattered around the three large objects, which all stuck up out of the muddy sea bottom and were obviously the three marks that had appeared on the sonar record. None of these large objects could be raised without special equipment, so they were left in place.

The divers did bring up some of the wooden objects that first day. There was a long curved piece with two holes in it, a straight piece about five feet long, and a piece with two cannonballs attached to it.

After examining the finds, Searle, Kunz, and Wyman theorized that the curved and straight pieces were part of the structure of a ship. The other object, which had been found next to one of the cannon-sized concretions, was probably a cannonball rack. When muzzle-loading cannons were used on sailing vessels, they were referred to as four-pounders, six-pounders, and eight-pounders. This designation meant that the cannon fired a cannonball of that particular weight. The cannonballs on the fragment of cannonball rack, or shot rack, were approximately three and one-quarter inches in diameter, the diameter of a ball weighing six pounds.

Actually, the balls weighed less than a pound. Most of the iron had been leached, or drawn out, because of the chemical reaction with the salt water. Only the substance known as graphite, which is much lighter than iron, was left.

Over the next few weeks, the student divers brought up a number of other objects, or artifacts, as archeologists refer to them, from the site. Most of them turned out to be associated with ships or warfare. Among them were

Above: A shot rack with cannonballs found early in the excavation.
Right: A team member cleans a wooden knee.
Structures like this once supported the deck beams.

more six-pound cannonballs, dark-green bottles, pulley blocks like those used in the rigging of sailing ships, and a large cylinder made from lead that had been used as a drainpipe, or scupper, to let water run off the deck. Another interesting find was a knee, an L-shaped piece of tree root that helped to support the deck. Knees were made from the curved roots of the hackmatack, or larch tree.

What the sonar project had located was apparently an old sailing ship, but where was the hull?

Some early finds from the *Defence*.

It was hidden from view, deeply buried beneath the mud seabed. To remove the mud, faculty members and students constructed a thirty-foot-long air lift. An air lift works something like a vacuum cleaner and is often used to clear sand or mud from shipwrecks. This one was made from PVC plastic pipe, a garden hose, and a small air compressor. One end of the hose is connected to the compressor. To "dig" with the air lift, a diver inserts the garden hose inside the pipe. Air from the compressor bubbles up the pipe to the surface. As the bubbles rise, they become larger and larger, creating suction. Soon mud is spurting from the top end of the pipe into the sieve.

As the mud was slowly cleared away, part of the hull came into view. The divers could see some of the wooden planking that covers the inside of the hull.

Now that they had a ship, the same question was on everyone's mind. Was this wreck one of the Penobscot Fleet? The best way to find out was to raise one of the large concretions and chip away the graphite to see what was inside. Cannon often have a date or some other identifying mark.

In the next several days, Wyman rigged a block and tackle on the Academy's fifty-foot workboat, the *Challenger*. When the boat was anchored over the wreck site, divers went down and attached two slings of manila line around the concretion. The block and tackle pulled up the graphite mass until it was just above the water off the boat's stern. Then the mass was lashed to the stern.

While this operation was going on, a fog had rolled in and the water in the harbor had become choppy. Out in the Bay, the waves were much higher. To make sure the concretion wouldn't be lost, a buoy was put on it.

Wyman carefully charted a route back to Castine. The waves were five feet high in the Bay during the trip, but the *Challenger* and its cargo returned safely to Castine. When the concreted object was unloaded on the dock,

Above: The concreted mass was lashed to the stern.
Right: Penobscot Bay—an X indicates the location
of the wreck of the *Defence*.

the teachers and students stood around looking at it. "The more we looked at it, the less it looked like a cannon," remembers Wyman. "Someone said, 'Maybe it's a car axle.' We went to dinner, but we couldn't stop thinking about it. After dinner we all went back down to the dock and began chipping away at the concretion. After about an hour, out of the middle of it came a cannon."

The iron cannon, five feet eight inches long, was the size that uses six-pound balls. One trunnion—the part of the cannon that rests on the carriage—had a faint symbol indicating it had been cast in Massachusetts. Mayhew's research showed that the *Defence* had been launched in

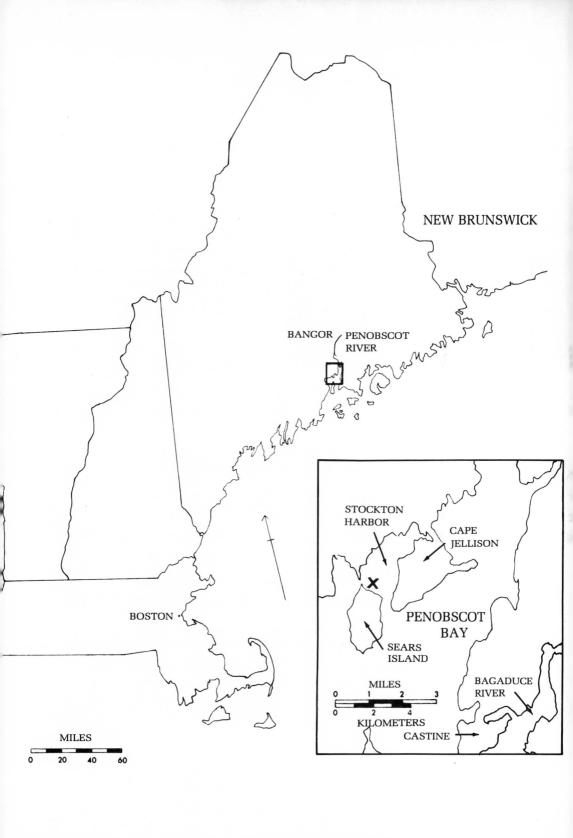

NEW BRUNSWICK

BANGOR   PENOBSCOT
RIVER

BOSTON ·

MILES

0   20   40   60

STOCKTON
HARBOR

CAPE
JELLISON

✕

PENOBSCOT
BAY

SEARS
ISLAND

MILES

0   1   2   3

0   2   4

KILOMETERS

BAGADUCE
RIVER

CASTINE →

1778 or 1779 and that its guns had been cast in Massachusetts. This cannon could well have been one of the
sixteen six-pounders that she had been carrying. After
almost two hundred years the *Defence* had been found.

3

Exploring the Wreck

Teams of students and teachers from the Maine Maritime Academy and MIT explored the wreck of the *Defence* during the next two summers of 1973 and 1974. Under a recent state law, the Maine State Museum is responsible for all archeological sites within the state, so Captain William Searle had received permission from the Museum to conduct a preliminary investigation. By this time, the *Defence* project had been given a name: Heritage Restored. The name proved to be a good one as more and more information about seafaring during the Revolution began to accumulate.

The divers working with the air lift removed mud and silt, revealing the outline of the hull. The brick structure turned out to be located behind the stump of the foremast near the bow. When they uncovered more of it, they realized that it had been the galley cookstove. The four brick walls supported a large, square copper caldron. Nearby were two copper pot covers. The pots, however, were not found. The cook may have taken them ashore just before the *Defence* was burned.

Other food-related artifacts also turned up in the bow. There were numerous barrel staves, animal bones, and a whole earthenware pitcher. The bones were later identified as coming from a cow. Searle and Wyman speculated that they must be what was left of the ship's stores. Salted beef was one of the staples of a sailor's diet back in the 1700's. Another item found in this area was a small wooden bucket. Scratched on the bottom were the letters AK. They may have been the initials of one of the sailors who served on the *Defence*.

The largest artifact brought up during this period was the second cannon that had been left in the wreck. When its covering of eroded iron and marine growth was chipped away back in Castine, it measured five feet long, about eight inches shorter than the first cannon. On one trunnion was stamped the date 1778. Still attached to the cannon were the remains of the wooden carriage on which the gun was mounted. The wood was badly deteriorated.

Dean Mayhew inspected the cannon and carriage and found, to his surprise, that the cannon mount appeared

Two views of the galley cookstove and caldron: above,
an underwater photograph; below, Peter Hentschel's drawing.

Left: The second cannon being unloaded in Castine.
Above: The trunnion has the date 1778.

to be very different from the standard Revolutionary War naval type. The carriage enabled the gunner to swing the gun around in a circle. During the Revolutionary period, cannon usually fired straight ahead. In order to point the gun at an enemy vessel, the helmsman had to turn the ship so that the gun faced the target. Mayhew's idea was that this particular cannon may have been mounted so that it could be pointed easily in different directions. The exact way the carriage worked, however, is still a mystery that remains to be solved.

Another mystery was the identity of a scoop-shaped piece of lead with jagged teeth cut into one end. At first, the excavation team thought it was a tool to clean the ashes from the stove's firebox. Later, thanks to information provided by the Smithsonian Institution in Washington, D.C., they learned that it was a vent cover for a cannon. Rare today, vent covers were used to cover the touchhole, where the cannon was fired by lighting a match that ignited the gunpowder. The vent cover kept the powder dry so the cannon was ready for firing.

By the end of the summer of 1974, hundreds of artifacts had been recovered and transported to the Maine State Museum at Augusta. There they were stored in water-filled tanks to await preservation treatment. Enough mud had been cleared from the hull to reveal that much of the original structure was still intact. When they reviewed the progress of the excavation, Searle and Wyman became convinced that the wreck was indeed the *Defence*. Information learned from her, they realized, would make an important contribution to nautical archeology.

In 1974, nautical archeology, the scientific study of shipwrecks and other maritime remains, was a brand-new field of study. Formerly, divers who found wrecks were interested only in their contents, particularly treasure. Nautical archeologists are interested in the contents of wrecks too, but not because of their monetary value. To them, the value of the artifacts lies in the clues they provide to a better understanding of what happened in the past. Nautical archeologists work with extreme care and record everything they find in hopes of reconstructing the events of hundreds or thousands of years ago.

They are also very interested in learning as much as possible about how ships are built. Many secrets of past shipbuilding can be learned from the painstaking investigation of what remains of the hull of a sunken vessel.

The *Defence* would be of particular interest to nautical archeologists because only one other Revolutionary War vessel, the *Philadelphia*, has been found in the waters of the United States. (It was raised from Lake Champlain and today is on display at the Smithsonian Institution in Washington, D.C.) As a result, little is known about how American ships were constructed in Colonial times. Information learned from the *Defence* would fill in many gaps. Furthermore, the artifacts found with the wrecked privateer would give a clearer picture of how American seamen lived during the Revolutionary War era.

Searle was on the board of directors of the American Institute of Nautical Archeology or AINA. (A few years later the name was changed to the Institute of Nautical Archeology or INA.) The president of the Institute is Dr. George Bass. Until then, the Institute had been involved only in the excavation of ancient shipwrecks in the Mediterranean. When Searle wrote Bass about the *Defence*, he immediately became interested in the possibility of investigating a shipwreck close to home. One of his plans was to establish a summer field school to train college students in the methods of nautical archeology. The *Defence*, he realized, might make a good site for a field school.

After Bass returned to the United States from Turkey, where he had been working on the excavation of an ancient vessel, he contacted Dr. David C. Switzer, a history professor at Plymouth State College in New Hampshire. Switzer had worked in Turkey with Bass and was learning the methods used in nautical archeology. Bass described the *Defence* to Switzer and asked him to visit the site with him that winter.

Bass and Switzer arrived in Castine on a cold January day in 1975. Snow was falling as David Wyman piloted the Academy boat *Panthalass* to Stockton Harbor with the two visitors aboard. They both donned wetsuits and dived into the icy water. Academy students gave them a quarter-hour tour of the wreck. The nautical archeologists saw enough to be very impressed. Back in Castine, Searle, Bass, Switzer, and Wyman sat around a wood-stove fire at the Wyman house, looking at photographs of the artifacts and discussing the wreck. Everyone was enthusiastic about the possibility of a scientific excavation.

That spring INA agreed to undertake a survey of the wreck in the summer of 1975. David Switzer would be director and David Wyman codirector. The Maine State Museum and the Maine Maritime Academy would be part of the project too. INA would be in charge of the archeological work and would hold a field school. The Museum would be responsible for the artifacts, and the Academy would furnish a base of operations and equipment.

If all went well during the survey, the participants

David Switzer.

planned a full-scale excavation for the following summer.

The 1975 survey had two goals. One was to learn how much of the *Defence* was actually intact. The other was to estimate how many artifacts remained. For the Museum, the second goal was particularly important, because its conservation laboratory was not equipped to work on large numbers of waterlogged artifacts. When it had an idea of how many there were, it would know how much equipment and how many people would be needed to support a full-fledged excavation.

The survey began in the first week of June. Switzer's first order of business was to arrange for a twenty-by-forty-foot float to be towed to Stockton Harbor and anchored over the wreck. On the float was a small shack with a stove and drawing table. Working from a float was much easier than working from a boat, because there was plenty of room for the compressors and other equipment needed in the excavation of an underwater site.

As soon as they made the first dive, the staff and students encountered a major problem: visibility. It was so poor that they continually lost their way groping through the murky water. As the staff discussed the problem, Bass described the frame that he had built over the wreck he had excavated in Turkey.

"Let's do the same thing here," he suggested. "It

David Wyman.

Above: The work float in 1975.
Below: This site plan shows a grid over the midship section.
Letters and numbers identify the squares.

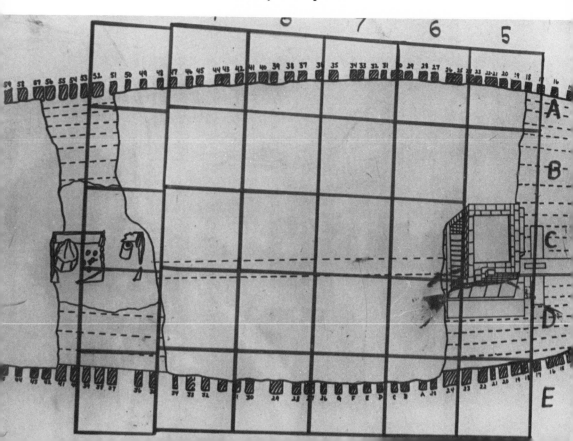

should make the poor visibility less of a problem."

The team obtained PVC pipe and used it to construct a grid of six five-foot squares. It was lowered over the bow, the site of the first test excavation. The grid rested about eight inches above the wreck on legs sunk deep into the mud. It worked. The divers could easily see the white pipe, and they could rest on it when they were operating the air lift or doing other work. From then on, a grid was used wherever the divers were working.

Mud was another major problem. To remove it from the wreck, the team used an air lift, like the earlier excavators. The air lift emptied onto a kind of floating sieve anchored a little distance away from the float. The earlier excavators had used a floating sieve too, but the new model had several improvements. The new sieve had a name: Priscilla. One of the team members sat on Priscilla and carefully examined the mud and silt for any small artifacts that might have come up through the pipe.

Dave Switzer's plan for the summer's work was to com-

A team member sifts debris on Priscilla.

plete three test trenches—one in the bow, one in the mid-ship area, and one in the stern of the ship. Enough of the ship would be uncovered for Dave Wyman to begin a plan of the hull. Making the plan involved placing num-bered tags on each of the ribs, or frames, and then using tape measures to record their exact position. The process is called triangulation. Dave Wyman used this informa-tion to begin a plan of the hull structure.

The wreck turned out to be about seventy feet long and twenty feet wide at the widest point. It lay more on the port side than on the starboard. From the bow to the stump of the mainmast, the hull was intact. In the stern area, however, the timbers were in a confusing jumble, like a giant jackstraw game. Dave Switzer agreed with his partner that the destruction of the stern was probably the result of the explosion of the magazine that sent the *Defence* to the bottom.

Using a metal probe rod, Switzer and a field-school student tested the depth of the mud in various locations. It varied from three to four or five feet. Beneath it, they hit the stones that made up the ballast.

As the survey team explored the hull, they also estimated the number of artifacts that would be un-covered when the real excavation began. In the bow, test trenches revealed barrels. Part of a shoe and a bone whistle turned up in another trench. The mainmast area yielded what seemed to be a large box. Nearby were grapeshot stools, or spindles, small wooden discs with a peg in the middle. In the Revolutionary War era, grape-shot, a kind of cannon ammunition used to destroy the

54

rigging of enemy ships, was packed around these spindles and tied in place. The excavators plunged their hands beneath the mud over the box and felt what seemed to be cannonballs. More balls rested in a long rack nearby. In all, about two hundred artifacts were brought up, numbered, and recorded.

Bass, Wyman, and Switzer hoped to be able to take photographs of the wreck, but none of the photographs were clear because of the poor visibility. So divers had to

A grapeshot stool or stand, grapeshot balls,
and a fragment of the original covering of coarse fabric.

draw what they saw. One weekend Peter Hentschel, the husband of one of the staff members, visited the site. An architect trained in drawing, Hentschel dived and produced excellent drawings of the site. The staff was so enthusiastic about his efforts that Hentschel became a weekend member of the staff. His drawings recorded most of the wreck's features.

To draw the parts of the wreck, Hentschel dived with a sheet of mylar plastic on a clipboard and an ordinary lead pencil. He quickly sketched the various features and later translated the sketches into finished drawings.

An early plan of the *Defence.*

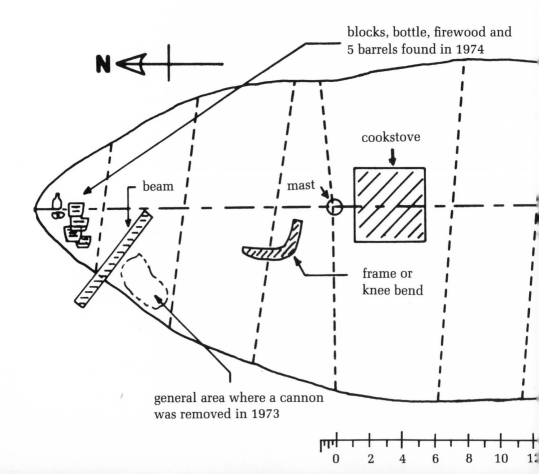

N

blocks, bottle, firewood and 5 barrels found in 1974

cookstove

beam

mast

frame or knee bend

general area where a cannon was removed in 1973

0   2   4   6   8   10   1

When the survey was completed on July 15, Switzer and Wyman had a good idea of what was left of the *Defence*. Basically it was the lower hull. All of the structure above the deck and most of the deck itself had vanished. But about 40 to 50 percent of the hull was still intact beneath the waters of Stockton Harbor, more than the remains of any other Revolutionary ship in the United States with the exception of the *Philadelphia*. In addition, the wreck contained many well-preserved artifacts, most of them lying almost where they had sunk on the night of August 14, 1779. Thus, each artifact could be related to a particular part of the ship.

As Dave Switzer noted in his report on the survey, the

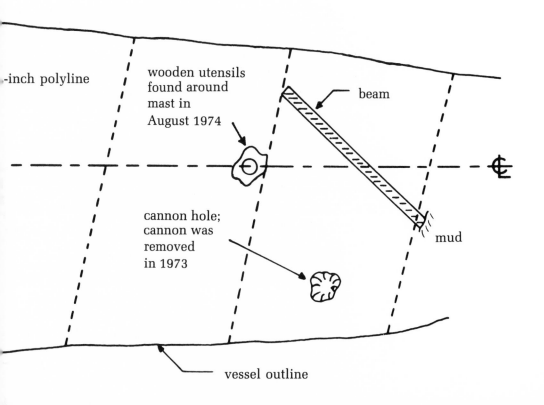

Defence was a "Revolutionary War time capsule."

What kept the *Defence* and its artifacts in such good condition for 200 years?

The mud was certainly a major factor. Mud and silt created an anaerobic condition; that is, there was no oxygen. Lack of oxygen cut down or eliminated organisms such as worms that feed on organic material—wood, leather, and bone. Another factor in the preservation of the *Defence* was the speed with which she sank, limiting the damage caused by fire. Finally, the wreck site had never been plundered by unthinking sport divers, so that the artifacts within the hull were undisturbed.

During the fall and winter months following the survey, plans for the full-scale excavation were developed. The Maine State Museum bought equipment and chemicals necessary for treating waterlogged artifacts. Someone trained in conservation, the institution decided, should be on hand at the wreck site to take charge of the artifacts as they were brought up. INA announced a second field school at the *Defence* site. Switzer and Wyman discussed excavation strategy.

The excavation would begin in the summer of 1976, the bicentennial year of the Declaration of Independence. What better year to begin the excavation of a Revolutionary War privateer?

4

A
1779
Time Capsule

Dave Switzer and Dave Wyman knew after the 1975 survey that there would be many artifacts within the hull of the *Defence*. The artifacts are valuable because they are rare objects, of course, but they are important for another reason too. They tell us something of a sailor's life in the 1700's. Some of this information can be gleaned from where the artifact is found. If a plate or bowl is lying in a certain area, for instance, it suggests that the seamen might have eaten their meals nearby.

To obtain as much information as possible from the artifacts, Switzer set up an artifact recovery system in

1976 before the excavation began. First the staff made a grid to set up over the area to be excavated, just as they had done in 1975. The 1976 grid was much bigger than the earlier one. It measured twenty feet on each side and had twenty-five five-foot squares. Each square was numbered, and each row of five squares was given a letter. Square number three in the first row, for example, was A3.

The grid was positioned over the bow in 1976. Each year it was moved to the next area to be excavated. Positioning the grid was hard work, because it had to be level.

When an artifact was located, its position within the

Field-school students build a grid frame.

grid square was recorded by the excavator on a drawing board. The excavator also noted the distance from the grid down to the artifact. This figure was known as the DBD, for depth below datum. The datum, or reference point, was the grid. Because the visibility was so poor, the excavator might miss an object and it would go up the air lift. To make sure the position of these finds too would be recorded, one team member on the float always kept track of where the air lift was operating.

After each artifact was brought up to the float, it was cataloged on a special card by the Museum conservation specialist. The card gave each artifact a number and provided information on where it was found, who found

An artifact card was used to catalog each object;
the log book recorded the daily recovery of the finds.

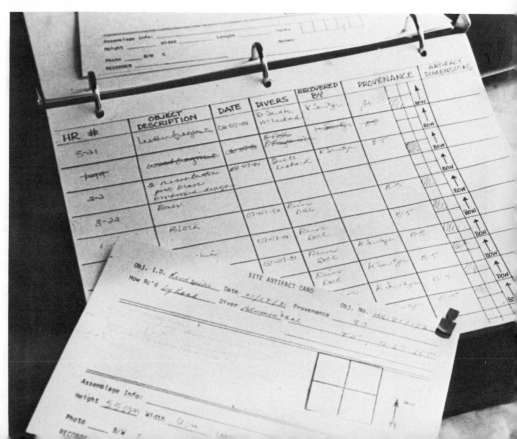

it, and, if it was known, what it was. There was also a space to draw a picture of the artifact. Later, at the Museum, notes were added to show how it had been treated. The cards were filed in categories according to what the artifact was made of: metal, wood, leather, etc.

By the time the excavation of the *Defence* was completed, there were some 3,000 cards. They did not represent 3,000 complete artifacts, however. On some cards, only a small fragment, such as a shard of glass, was described. One reconstructed bottle might be represented by as many as sixty cards.

Switzer's overall plan for excavating the *Defence* was to begin work in the bow. The excavators were to tackle the forward part of the bow in 1976 and then work backward as far as they could. The following summer, the excavation would be extended into the middle portion of the hull. The stern would be left until last. Switzer estimated that five summer seasons would be needed to clear the wreck. As it turned out, he was right on target.

The bow excavation got under way in June of 1976. The work took on a rhythm as the days passed. Every day, six days a week, the student excavators put on the wet suits required by the cold Maine water, wriggled into

Switzer and two visitors inspect artifacts
in the water-filled tubs as Betty Seifert and Jon Blumenfeld
catalog other artifacts on a table in the rear.

scuba gear, picked up their equipment—drawing boards and trays to hold the artifacts—and jumped into the water. They worked in teams of two, supervised by an INA member who was an experienced diver. On the bottom, the teams examined one grid at a time, manipulating the air lift to remove the mud.

Even the difficult chore of removing the ballast proceeded according to a system. Bucket lines were set up from the float down to the wreck, where the ballast removal teams filled the buckets with the smaller rocks on the top level. A pull on the line was the signal for the

Everyone had a job on the work float.
In the center is the floating sieve.
Buoys mark the position of the wreck.

Workers on the float search through bottom debris
for artifacts airlifted from the wreck.

float team to pull up a loaded bucket and send down an
empty one. The larger ballast stones on the lower level—
some weighed more than fifty pounds—were dropped in
a pile on the starboard side of the wreck. By 1979, the
pile was nearly five feet high.

Up on the float, team members looked through the
ballast for any small artifacts or pieces of artifacts that
might have been overlooked. The stones were kept for

later return to the wreck. Another team member examined the air-lifted debris in the floating sieve.

The first thing the divers came across as they explored the bow were numerous loose barrel staves. As they penetrated deeper with the air lift, they uncovered intact barrels. Almost nothing else was found in the front part of the bow. Switzer was surprised by the large number of barrels, because he had expected that this part of the bow would have been a place where at least some of the crew slept. But it was apparently a provision area. The intact barrels would have collapsed if they had been raised to the surface, so they were taken apart and removed in pieces. First, however, each stave was numbered and drawn in situ (in place), so the barrels could be reassembled.

The contents of the barrels turned out to be remnants of salt beef and pork, the same food identified earlier on the wreck. There was nothing surprising about finding so much of this kind of food, since it made up the major portion of the sailor's diet at that time. Meat was salted or pickled to keep it from spoiling. On board ship, it was boiled for a long time to make it palatable, but even then it wasn't very tasty. Sailors often called it "salt horse."

Working backward from the bow, the divers came to the stove area. There were so many artifacts there that they needed part of three summers to bring them all up. Most of them were tools, objects associated with firing cannons, or personal items belonging to the crew. The variety suggests that the stove, or galley, area was a very busy place when the ship was under sail. The bos'un

A rammer was used to push wadding into the cannon.

(the man who had charge of all of the shipboard work), the carpenter, and the gunner probably all had compartments there, judging from the tools found. They included a fid, a wooden tool used in splicing rope; a leather sailmaker's palm to protect the hand when sewing sails; a number of wooden handles for tools (the iron tools themselves had crumbled away); and a rammer used to push cannonballs and balls of hemp called wadding into the cannon. Wadding kept the balls in place.

Almost all the clothing consisted of items like shoes, shoe buckles, and buttons which had the best chance of surviving 200 years in salt water and mud. Some of the shoes were still intact, although most were squashed flat by the mud. After being treated and stitched back together at the Maine State Museum, they still looked wearable—for someone with very small feet. Most of them were about the size of a man's size-three shoe today.

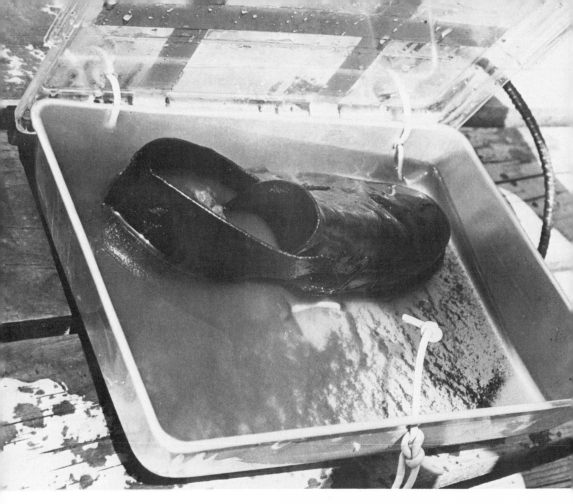

Above: A leather shoe in a water-filled tray on the float. The shoe was in good condition when it was brought up from the wreck.
Below: This military button was found in the stove area.

One of the most interesting buttons found in the stove area was made of pewter and had the initials USA. It undoubtedly belonged to a uniform, possibly worn by one of the soldiers evacuated before the retreat.

A few less substantial items of clothing also survived. A silk ribbon was found, still tied. Later tests at the Museum showed it was green in color. The ribbon was probably tied around one of the flat-brimmed hats sailors wore in the eighteenth century. A mass of fabric was found aft of the stove in 1978, and when it was analyzed at the Museum, it proved to be linen. It had some wooden buttons on it and may have been a shirt or some other article of clothing.

Most of the other personal items found in the stove area were connected with food. They included a wooden

This piece of ribbon was still tied when it was recovered.

Among the personal items uncovered were a wooden plate, or trencher, and a wooden spoon.

bowl, a wooden platter called a trencher, a pewter plate, many pewter spoons, a ceramic mug missing only the handle, a green rum bottle, and a number of wooden staves about a foot long. At first, the staff thought the staves were the remains of washtubs, but Switzer later learned that they were the remnants of a mess kid. A kid was a small bucket in which the sailors' food was served. On ships of the Revolutionary War era, sailors were grouped into mess sections of six or seven men. Each section had a kid; each messmate had a bowl, mug, and spoon. The mess captain doled out portions to the sections from the kid.

One complete mess kid was found near the stove. The complete kid and the other kid remains had different marks (archeologists call them "graffiti") scratched on them. Among the marks noted on other kid remains were X's, stars, and circles. There were initials on the kids too: AD, AK, J.B. Dave Switzer speculates that the initials are those of the men who served as mess captains. If so, J.B. had a sense of history. On the base of his kid, he not only carved his initials but the date, 1779. Apart from the cannon, this object was the only one that gave a date for the wreck.

More initials were found on the bowls and handles of the spoons. Some of the spoons were bent and twisted—possibly from the heat of the fire that burned before the ship sank—but others were almost like new.

"These spoons look like they've just been taken out of a drawer," remarked Switzer when he saw them.

Where were all these artifacts kept on the crowded ship when it was under sail?

The date 1779 was scratched on the bottom of this mess kid. The initials may be those of a mess section leader.

Above: Most pewter spoons were found in excellent condition. This one came from the stove area.

Below: A pewter plate nine inches in diameter. The marks of a knife can be seen, but no one knows what made the hole.

In 1978, a pile of long boards was found near the stove. Personal belongings and galley equipment lay between the boards. Switzer believes that they may have been shelves where the cook kept his supplies and the crew members placed their bowls, spoons, and even items of clothing.

One group of artifacts found near the stove was not easy to identify. They were small wooden tags carved in a number of different shapes. All had notches cut in them, and most had graffiti such as X's or initials, including AD. Everyone on the excavation team puzzled over the tags. Switzer suggested that they represented a kind of talley to be hung on a board: a "meal ticket," as it were. Another member of the staff speculated that the tags were pieces of a game that the sailors played.

The solution to the mystery came from the Mariners Museum in Newport News, Virginia. According to Larry Gilmore, assistant curator of the Department of Collections, tags like these identified a mess section. A string was tied to the tag, and it was attached to a piece of salt beef or pork before it was put in the stove caldron to be boiled. When the meat was ready to be served, the leaders of the mess section identified their chunks of meat by the tag, pulled them out of the caldron, and carried them to their messmates.

The stove itself was the largest artifact in the galley area and, in fact, in the entire wreck. Five feet high, five feet wide, and five feet deep, it was sheathed in wide pine boards and rested on a wooden platform. The copper stove caldron fitted so neatly inside it that

Wooden mess tags identified portions of meat for a mess section.

Switzer and Wyman believe it might have been made for the stove. When they examined the caldron in 1976, they realized that it was deteriorating. After checking with Stephen Brooke, the Maine State Museum conservator, Switzer decided to bring the caldron to the surface so it could be treated at the Museum.

Bringing up the heavy, water-filled artifact was a big operation. Shelley Reisman, the conservation specialist who worked on the float, built a special box with a cradle inside to hold the caldron for shipment to Augusta. After it was ready, Switzer and Rhys Townsend, a student staff member, tied a lift bag—an air-filled plastic bag—to the caldron and put a line around it. With four people pushing from below and others pulling from above, the caldron rose slowly to the surface.

Once the caldron was up on the float, Shelley Reisman quickly wrapped it in burlap to protect it. Then she and other staff members lifted it onto the cradle inside the box. The caldron had not been exposed to the air for more than five or six minutes.

Back in Castine, the box was filled with fresh water so that the caldron could begin the long process of leaching out the salt. The caldron spent another year and a half in treatment at the Museum. Today the sixty-eight gallon container is in excellent condition.

After the excavation was over in 1976, and in each of the following field seasons, the field-school students spent the last few days covering up the wreck to preserve the anaerobic conditions. Then ballast stones that had been brought up were bagged and dropped down into the

wreck. Polyethylene sheets were spread over any exposed structures and stapled in place. In later years, sand was dumped over the entire excavation. In 1978, a special sand-carrying craft was designed and built by the Maine Maritime Academy summer students to cover the *Defence*. It made the job much easier.

The caldron was brought to the surface
after a great deal of work.

5

Life on the *Defence*

After one summer season had been completed, David Switzer realized that he would have to speed up the work of uncovering the seventy or so feet of vessel that remained. So he set up a two-team approach with two air lifts. While one team worked in the bow, another team worked in the midship area. A dive master and a recorder, both full-time positions, were added to the staff. The dive master planned the dives and made sure strict safety procedures were followed. The recorder kept a daily journal.

Most of the excavators in 1977 and 1978 were field-school students, just as they had been in 1975 and 1976. By this time, INA was permanently based at Texas A&M University, where George Bass and his associates offered a number of courses in nautical archeology. Many of the students who took these courses in the middle and late 1970's signed up for the *Defence* field school and got their first field experience excavating the Revolutionary War privateer.

As the excavation moved to the mainmast area in 1977 and 1978, more and more artifacts came to light. There

Nancy Orton, leader of the group working around the mainmast in 1978, and Dave Switzer discuss the work her team is carrying out in grid 10.

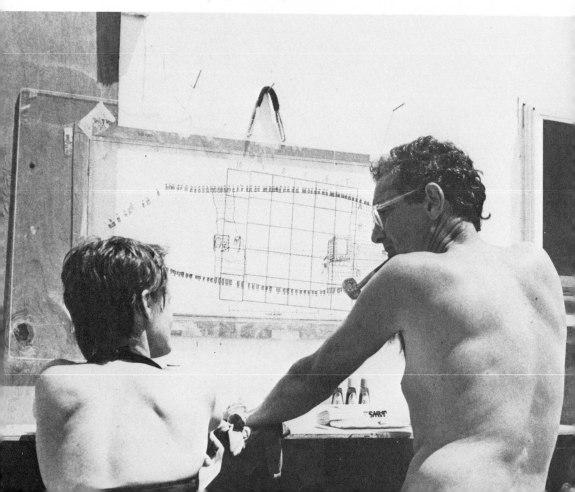

were no cannons, but there were a number of objects used in firing the cannon. One of them was a hand spike. An oaken staff like a crowbar, it was used to raise and lower the cannon barrel or to move the carriage so that the gunner could take better aim. Other finds connected with the cannon were the wheels for a carriage, a wedge used to raise or lower the barrel, and a wooden plug called the tompion that is placed in the muzzle to keep out seawater.

The large box with grapeshot stools in the mainmast area, which was first seen in 1975, wasn't completely free of mud until 1978. It turned out to be six feet long, three feet wide, and four feet high. Inside were cannonballs and grapeshot. Obviously the box was the shot locker. Actually, only half of the box held ammunition; the rest of it was empty except for a wooden pipe. To Switzer and Wyman, this empty part was clearly the remains of the bilge pump and the pump well that kept the lower hull, or bilge, free of water. From the well, the pipe would have extended to the deck above.

Very little is known about shot lockers of the Revolutionary War period, so Dave Switzer wanted to examine it closely. But the poor visibility made the details of the box difficult to see.

Switzer and Nancy Orton, the leader of the group working around the mainmast in 1978, inspected the box and found that it would not be hard to take apart and put back together again. But would the Museum have room for it? Switzer checked with Stephen Brooke, who said yes. The removal of the shot locker went smoothly.

Left: Team leader Cynthia Orr pours water on a large oak piece as Carol Olsen takes measurements for a drawing.
This piece may be part of a gun carriage.
Above: This underwater photograph shows the grapeshot stools in the shot locker.
Below: Peter Hentschel sketched the shot locker. The mainmast stump is at the right, the bilge pump pipe at the left.

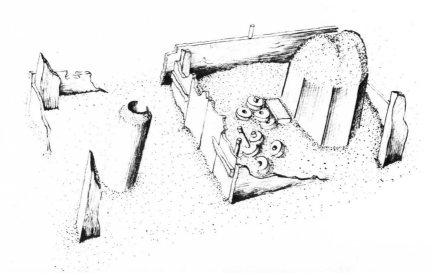

Orton's team tagged and numbered each piece, then drew them *in situ*. Switzer, meanwhile, had fashioned some wooden wedges. When the box had been sketched, he and Orton used the wedges to pry the boards gently apart, one by one. The excavators took them up to the float, where Orton's team reassembled the box again.

In the bright sunlight on the float, Switzer could see the saw marks on the pine boards. They were evenly spaced and vertical, which meant that they were cut by a mechanical saw with a blade that went up and down. Such up-and-down saws were common in Colonial New England. They were usually powered by water.

The locker boards were reassembled on the float.

Switzer also noted that some of the boards were mismatched and had an irregular nail pattern. There were notches on the bottom of the structure to make it fit on the bottom of the vessel, but the notches were not centered. When it was in place, the structure probably was a little off center. All these observations suggested to Switzer that the locker might have been an example of hasty construction. He speculated that the locker might have been enlarged at the last minute to carry the cannonballs given to the privateer when she joined the Penobscot Expedition.

The mainmast area wasn't used only for naval supplies. There were numerous barrel staves there too, suggesting that it was a provision area like the front part of the bow. One of the parts was unusual. It was the end of a barrel and on it was a label of the contents: *Pork 32 Pieces Ea Ford.*

Artifacts found in the area between the mainmast and the stove were more personal. They included wooden tankards with initials and marks, a clay pipe with teeth marks, liquor bottles, a pewter plate, and more shoes, buttons, and buckles. Two small bottles with stoppers were discovered among the ballast stones. As one of the field-school students picked up the bottles, a strong aroma wafted over the float.

"Smells like mothballs," remarked someone.

The smell was coming from the bottles, one of which still had liquid inside. The liquid was later analyzed and proved to be pine oil, which was used by physicians in the eighteenth century as a medicine. Dave Switzer be-

lieves that these small bottles were part of the ship's medicine chest.

These personal items suggest that the area between the stove and mainmast was probably where the crew bunked. The best evidence for this conclusion were two artifacts that looked like parts of a hammock. One was a flat piece of wood with a line of holes in it. There were fragments of twine in each hole. The other was a piece of canvas. The wooden piece was thought to be a support for a hammock like those used by Colonial seamen, while the canvas was part of the hammock itself.

Another group of artifacts found in this same area played an important role in the navigation of the *Defence*. One looked like a ruler, and Switzer immediately recognized it as a Gunter scale, a kind of primitive computer. A navigator used the scale, which has numbers on both sides, to figure time and distance problems. Not far away from the scale were two wooden ob-

Left: Dave Switzer and Nancy Orton examine pieces of a tankard. The base has initials carved in it.
Below: A hammock remnant from the midship area suggests that this area served as the crew's sleeping quarters.

This wooden object found on the *Defence* is part
of a Davis quadrant, an early navigation instrument.

jects. At first, the excavators were puzzled about their
use, but Nancy Orton solved the mystery. When she was
reading a book on early navigation instruments, she discovered that the objects were part of a Davis quadrant. A
forerunner of the modern sextant, the Davis quadrant was
used to establish a vessel's position with regard to lati-
tude by measuring the height of the sun.

As Switzer and Wyman had expected, there were few
artifacts in the stern area, which was excavated in 1979.
But some of those found in and near the stern were sig-
nificant. One was a shoe made on a last (a form shaped
like the human foot) for the right foot. In the Colonial
period, such shoes were fairly expensive as most were
made to fit either foot. Brass buttons of the type found in
the stern would have been expensive then too. Finally, a
small teapot made of fine china was found in pieces. It
was later reassembled by the Museum, and the design
and color pattern resemble that in Whieldon ware, a kind
of fine china.

What these better-quality artifacts suggested to Dave Switzer was that they may have belonged to officers, whose quarters would have been in the stern. A pine board that looked like the end of a sea chest, a storage chest for personal belongings, also turned up in the stern. It could have belonged to either an officer or a crewman.

Bringing up the artifacts from the *Defence* was only the first step. As soon as they reached the float, a trained specialist in conservation took charge of them. The artifacts were immediately put in a tub of fresh water to prevent them from drying out and to keep the cell walls of organic items from collapsing. Each evening in Castine the conservation specialist and other members of the team carried the artifacts from the boat to the field

Immediately after being brought to Castine,
the artifacts were put in tubs of fresh water
in the field laboratory. Here ceramic pieces are being soaked.

laboratory. The laboratory was a large classroom in one of the buildings located near the waterfront.

In the laboratory, the artifacts were transferred to other water-filled tubs. They remained there until the conservation specialist or a Museum conservator could transfer them to the Maine State Museum's laboratory.

At the Museum, conservators examined each artifact and determined how to treat it. The goal of the Museum was not to make the artifacts look like new, but to preserve whatever remained of the original. In a number of cases, there was no known method of treatment because so little was known about artifacts that have been in salt water for long periods. "We learned as we went along," recalls Stephen Brooke. "The *Defence* project expanded the science of conservation."

A large laboratory had been set up in a building near the Museum to treat the *Defence* artifacts. Over the next five years, many conservators and technicians worked on the project. The first step for all the artifacts was soaking in deionized water—water from which chemical impurities have been removed—to take out the remaining salt. Afterward, each group was treated differently depending on what they were made of and their condition. Some were comparatively easy to treat, others were very difficult.

Faith Harrington works on a drawing of a pewter spigot that once fit into a barrel.

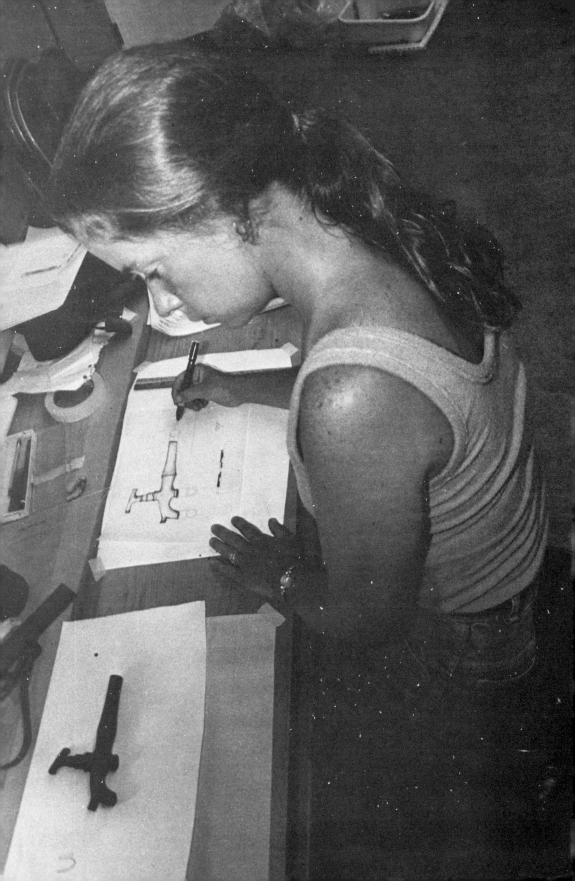

In general, artifacts made of pewter and ceramic (earthenware and china) were the easiest to treat, those made of iron and glass the hardest. Some iron and glass artifacts could not be treated successfully.

Artifacts made of leather and wood had to undergo a long, complex treatment, but they usually responded very well. These organic materials were first put in a freeze-dryer machine to remove all the moisture. Then they were soaked in water in which a compound called polyethylene glycol had been dissolved. Eventually the polyethylene glycol became part of the organic material

Artifacts were transferred from the field laboratory to the conservation laboratory at the Maine State Museum. Objects that have already undergone treatment are on the table in the foreground. Behind it are holding tanks. A freeze-dryer machine is at the right rear.

and stabilized whatever was left of the original structure.

Treatment of artifacts that have been in salt water for long periods takes time. By the end of the 1979 field season, the storage tanks at the Museum laboratory were overflowing with artifacts awaiting their turn. Some artifacts found in earlier years were still undergoing treatment. To give Stephen Brooke and his assistants time to catch up, Switzer and Wyman decided not to carry out an excavation in 1980. That summer was the first since 1972 that there had been no activity at the site.

The *Defence,* protected by sandbags and sand fill, awaited the excavation team's return in 1981.

6

The
Largest
Artifact

During the fall and winter months between field seasons, Dave Switzer prepared excavation reports. He often drove to Augusta from Plymouth, New Hampshire, where he teaches history at Plymouth State College, to examine the artifacts. Some had already undergone treatment, but others were still being held in water-filled tanks. For the most part, though, all except the most fragile finds could be examined. Careful handling was necessary as Switzer and Museum conservation technician Betty Seifert reached into the tanks to take out items.

Dave Switzer jots notes on the site plan.

The one artifact that could not be examined, of course, was the largest one of all—the hull of the *Defence*. But like the rest of the artifacts, it had to be inspected to understand how it had been constructed.

During the summer of 1976, Dave Switzer and Dave Wyman had talked about recovering the entire hull from the mud. The hull of the warship *Wasa*, which had sunk in the harbor in Stockholm, Sweden, in 1628, had been raised in 1961. She was about 200 feet long, much longer than what remained of the *Defence*. If the *Wasa* could be raised, the *Defence* could probably be raised too. Switzer and Wyman discussed their idea with the staff members of the Maine State Museum.

96

The prospect was exciting. But the more they talked, the more everyone realized that the task would be enormously expensive. The cost of the engineering involved in raising the wreck was only part of the story. Once free of the protective mud, the hull would have to be preserved like any other artifact. To do so would require a facility built especially for the job, a team of full-time conservators, and hundreds of gallons of polyethylene glycol. Although the project was receiving funding from the National Geographic Society and the Maine Historic Preservation Commission, the possibility of getting enough money to raise, treat, and preserve the hull was doubtful.

If the *Defence* had been a national treasure like the *Wasa* or our own *Constitution* (a United States Navy ship from the War of 1812 that has been preserved in Boston, Massachusetts), the prospects might have been better. However, even though the *Defence* was valuable in the eyes of nautical archeologists as the survivor of a naval disaster, she was hardly in the same class as the *Constitution.* Also, the *Defence,* unlike the *Wasa,* has undergone deterioration underwater. Her upper deck and other structures have long since fallen away. Faced with these realities, an alternative plan had to be found for the *Defence* by the members of Project Heritage Restored.

"If it isn't financially feasible to raise the wreck, what is the next best solution?" asked Stephen Brooke at a meeting of all the interested parties at the Museum in 1976.

The state archeologist suggested that the hull structure could be preserved by making detailed plans of all aspects of it. The participants were enthusiastic about the idea. By the time the meeting ended, a new phrase had been coined to describe the procedure of conserving the hull: "Preservation through documentation." It meant the recording of the hull by means of drawings, plans, a model, and, if possible, photographs.

Switzer and Wyman had already begun the process with the data they had collected. But now they needed even more detailed information. Dave Wyman was given the chief responsibility for getting it.

The clearing of the bow in 1977 gave Wyman his first opportunity to collect the information he needed to begin to draw a complete set of plans. The site plan he had already made gave a flat view of the structure. Now he needed to add a third dimension. Doing so meant obtaining cross-sectional measurements to show the shape *inside* the hull. Starting in the bow, Wyman selected locations where he would take these measurements.

The method he used was simple. A tape measure was stretched tightly across the hull. Then one person—often Dave Switzer—positioned a six-foot-long measuring stick at each foot along the tape. There was a carpenter's level

---

Dave Wyman transforms measurements
into drawings of the site plan.

on the stick to make sure it was vertical. Another person—usually Dave Wyman—moved the stick along the
tape and recorded the distance from the tape down into
the hull.

The method was simple, but obtaining the measurements of just one cross section often took as much as an
hour because of the poor visibility. By the end of the
hour, the measurement takers would come to the surface
shivering from the exposure to water temperature that
seldom rises above 50 degrees Fahrenheit.

After each dive, Dave Wyman went to his drawing
board in the float house and transformed the numbers on
his clipboard into drawings that showed the shape of the
hull. Peter Hentschel helped Wyman with the drawings
on weekend visits. Wyman also enlisted the aid of INA
ship reconstructor Richard Steffy, whose specialty was
building exact models of shipwrecked structures. Dick
Steffy came to Castine for three summers, and he and
Wyman spent many hours working on the plans.

Other information on the ship came to light gradually
as the excavation continued. She had been built almost
entirely of oak, including the frames, the interior

A cross-section profile of the hull showing the cookstove
and the extensive remains of the port side.

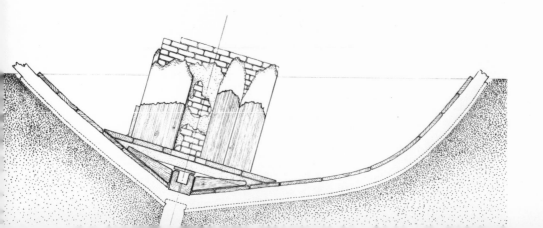

Peter Hentschel (center) spent weekends at the *Defence* site helping to sketch the wreck and its artifacts.

sheathing (which is called the ceiling), the outside plank-ing, and the beams that had supported the deck. The frames were made up of a number of pieces called fut-tocks, which were fastened together with oak pegs called trunnels or treenails. Trunnels also held the oak outside planking to the frames.

Pine or fir had been used for the decks as well as for the interior partitions. The masts had been made from tall white pine trees, but all that remained of them were five-foot stumps projecting a little above the seabed.

Dave Switzer and Dave Wyman inspected the mast stumps. The exposed parts were badly eroded, but be-

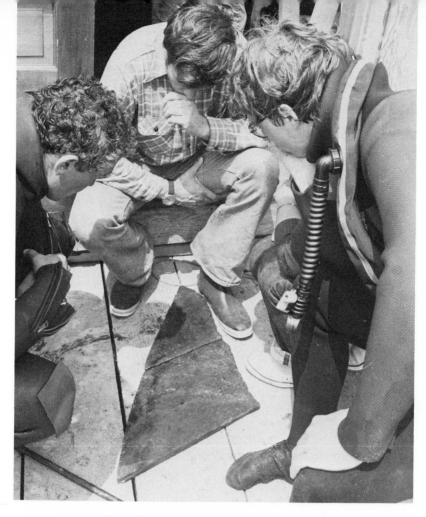

Dave Switzer, Dave Wyman, and student staff member
Rhys Townsend (left to right) examine what may be a remnant
of the bulkhead.

neath the mud they were surprisingly well preserved.
Wyman needed more information on the masts, including how they had been set into the keelson, the long
timber extending from bow to stern inside the ship. He
couldn't get what he wanted when the masts were in
place in the keelson, so plans were made to lift the foremast up to the float.

Rhys Townsend, now a student member of the staff,

dived down to the wreck and tied a lift bag to the foremast. Then he slowly filled the bag with air. Everyone had expected the waterlogged mast to be very heavy, but as the lift bag began to fill with air, the mast shuddered and rose quickly to the surface, taking a surprised Rhys along with it. Luckily, it was low tide and the water over the wreck was not deep. Sudden ascents can be very dangerous in diving. Once the mast was on the surface, it floated, much to the astonishment of Rhys and the rest of the excavation team.

"Let's get the measurements as quickly as possible, so we can replace it in the wreck," called out Dave Switzer.

The excavation team swung into action. While some members made measurements, drawings, and photographs of the stump, others fashioned a kind of harness out of lead weights and cinder blocks. The mast proved to be eighteen inches in diameter. A rule of thumb for old sailing ships says that each inch of diameter is equal to a yard in height. So the lower section of the *Defence's* foremast must have extended nearly fifty feet above the deck.

After the float work on the mast was completed, the harness of heavy weights was rigged around it and it was returned to the bottom. The harness, Switzer and Wyman believed, would keep the stump within the wreck.

They were wrong. The next day divers checked on the mast and found the weighted stump rising slowly out of the mud. Its buoyancy posed a problem. Dave Switzer called Stephen Brooke and explained the situation. Brooke agreed to accept the bulky artifact. So the stump was brought up once again, hauled onto the workboat,

Above: When the mast stump proved too buoyant
to stay underwater, it was brought up
and sent to the Maine State Museum.
Below: Cynthia Orr's drawing of the mast stump
shows its eight sides.

NORTH FACE

WEST FACE

FORE MAST HR176/1/261/1

SCALE 1"=1½"

CYNTHIA ORR 7/26/76

taken to Castine, and shipped off to Augusta. It would spend five years in a slow-dry treatment under conditions of controlled humidity and temperature. A special box had to be built to house it.

During the treatment, Brooke determined that the core of the mast was not waterlogged, which is why it was buoyant even after 200 years underwater.

After the bow of the *Defence* had been excavated, Wyman was able to reach some conclusions about how the vessel had been constructed. She had apparently been put together in what is called the whole mold method. That is, heavy frames called mold frames were set up every five feet or so along the keel, the long timber running the exterior length of the ship. These frames provided the basic shape of the hull. Once they were fastened to the keel, the lower outside planks were set in place. Then more frames were added in between the first ones to increase the hull's strength.

There was nothing unusual about this method of construction. It was common in the Colonial period. Just about everything Wyman had found out so far about the basic structure of the *Defence,* in fact, suggested she was a typical vessel of her type and period. Her major features corresponded to what has been written about Colonial ships. Very little, however, is known about the small yet important details of the way Colonial ships were put together. A number of these small details became clear as the hull of the *Defence* was uncovered.

One detail is the bark that remained on many of the ship's timbers. Whenever possible, it seems, the builder

of the *Defence* had followed the common practice of using naturally curved pieces of timber to make up the frames and other curved pieces. In the bow, the wishbone-shaped breasthook, which helped support the hull, had been made from the crotch of a tree. Wyman had expected this finding, but he had not expected to discover that bark was still attached to the breasthook. The same was true of many of the frames.

Was this practice common, or was it a sign of hasty construction?

Evidence of haste had already been found in the shot locker. Then, as Peter Hentschel was working on a drawing of the bow area, he found what looked like more sloppy workmanship. In his drawing, he was recording the position of the spikes that fastened the inner planking, or ceiling, to the frames. He was surprised to find

Left: Dave Wyman, Carol Olsen, and Lin Snow (left to right) inspect deck beam fragments and the knee.
Below: Only a few remnants remained of the deck planking.

that in many places the heavy planks were held by only a few nails. Some planks as long as twenty feet had only three iron spikes in them.

The lack of spikes could have been a result of too much haste in the building of the ship or of a shortage of iron. Iron was in short supply in the Colonies during the Revolution.

The jumble of timbers in the stern yielded more evidence of this kind. To enable Wyman to study these timbers more closely, some of them were lifted onto the float. A few were severely cracked, an indication that a powerful explosion had occurred nearby. Inspecting the stern timbers, Wyman found that the frames between the mold frames were not fastened to the keel at all. They were simply held in place by trunnels that went through the outside planking.

It may never be known for sure if this evidence indicates hasty workmanship or if there is some other explanation. Wyman believes, however, that the structural weaknesses in the *Defence* may have hastened her sinking. As he and Hentschel were examining the stern timbers, they realized that they should be able to find the keel in this part of the ship and record its measurements. They plunged probe rods into the mud where the keel should have been. Nothing.

An excavation team brought over an air lift and positioned it to dig. The air lift dug down nearly five feet, but again nothing was found.

Dave Switzer was as perplexed as Wyman and Hentschel. "If the entire stern had been blown away, I would

Dave Wyman examines timbers from the stern.

expect the keel to be missing, but not with all these timbers here," he said. "Let's keep looking."

The next day the mystery was partly solved. One of a
team of divers returning to the surface called out, "We've
found it!" About twelve feet behind the mainmast, at the
point where the keel had been severed, was a deep hole.
In the hole, the divers touched the broken end of the keel
that still remained attached to the hull. They probed all
around the hole, but failed to find the section of keel that
had broken away. It has never been found.

As the staff discussed the missing keel, Dave Wyman
speculated that if the *Defence* had been more solidly
framed, the explosion might not have caused this kind of

damage. Minus much of her keel, she must have sunk fairly quickly. For nautical archeology, however, the loss of the keel was a fortunate accident. If the *Defence* had been better able to withstand the blast, she would have floated longer and the fire would have burned more of her.

As it turned out, another fortunate accident had taken place on the *Defence* shortly after it sank. Near the port side of the bow, about twenty feet from the wreck, is a large piece of the ship's structure that somehow became separated from the rest of the vessel. It was found by accident, as no excavation has been done outside the wreck. Dave Switzer and student staff member Cynthia Orr dived down to examine it. They could see and feel a large timber with planks attached to it.

"I think it's a section of the hull," Switzer wrote on his clipboard.

The excavation team lifted the structure up to the float the next day. The late William Avery Baker and his wife, Ruth, were visiting the excavation that day. Bill Baker was the curator of the Russell Hart Nautical Museum at MIT and one of the foremost authorities on Colonial ship-building. He examined the timber and planking and pointed to a half-circle hole in the largest timber.

"I think that was the hawse hole where the anchor cable ran through," he said. "My guess is that this timber is part of the knighthead."

Knightheads were large frame timbers that stood on either side of the stem, the forward part of the bow. They were larger than any other frames in the bow. Dave

Divers confer about the latest artifact uncovered.

Wyman made a quick scale drawing of the timber and placed the drawing next to the plan of the bow. The size of the timber corresponded in size to the frame timber next to the stem on the port side. It was undoubtedly the knighthead. The knighthead and the planking attached to it enabled the *Defence* team to understand more about the outside covering of the ship and how it had been fastened to the frames.

By 1978, Dave Wyman had enough information on the hull to begin another plan, the plan of the profile. A profile shows the vessel from bow to stern as if one were standing off to one side. Wyman's profile stressed the port side. Because of the list, or tilt, of the wreck, the port side had more intact structure preserved by the mud.

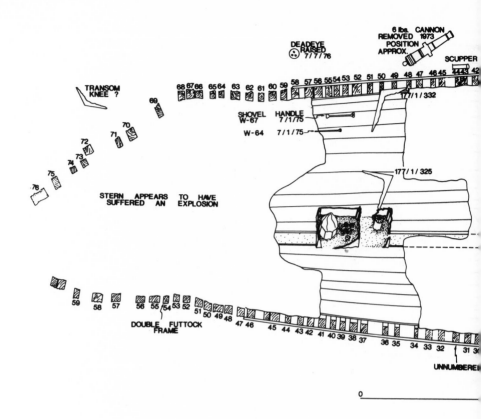

Dave Wyman's 1978 site plan shows the excavated bow,
the trench dug across the mainmast area,
and the location of some of the artifacts and structural features.

While he was working on the profile, Peter Hentschel
completed a perspective view of the bow and a detailed
plan, or flat view, of the bow.

Studying the profile plan and other plans for the
Defence, Wyman was able to get some idea of what kind
of vessel she was.

112

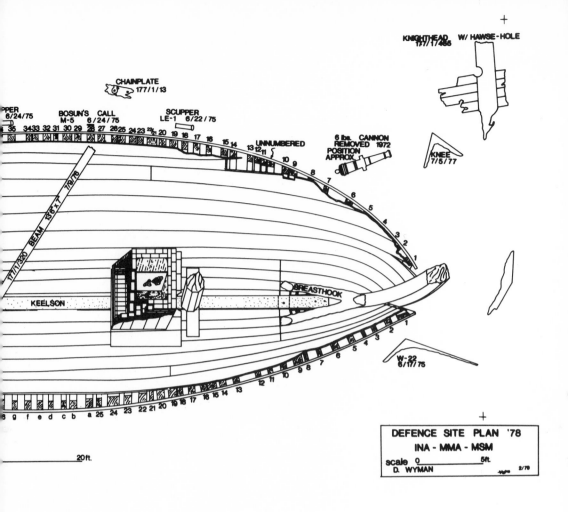

CHAINPLATE 177/1/13

KNIGHTHEAD W/ HAWSE-HOLE
177/1/485

PPER
6/24/75

BOSUN'S CALL
M-5   6/24/75

SCUPPER
LE-1   6/22/75

UNNUMBERED

6 lbs. CANNON
REMOVED 1972
POSITION
APPROX

KNEE
7/5/77

BEAM 136"×7 7/9/78

T7/1/320

KEELSON

BREASTHOOK

W-22
6/17/75

20ft.

DEFENCE SITE PLAN '78
INA - MMA - MSM
scale 0   5ft.
D. WYMAN   2/79

113

7

The
Last of
the *Defence*

The final excavation season on the *Defence* was scheduled for the summer of 1981. Between the 1979 and 1981 seasons, the Museum conservation laboratory was a busy place. As artifacts came out of treatment, they were replaced by others waiting in holding tanks. The freeze-dryer machine operated constantly. Some wooden objects, such as the tool handles, did not go into the freeze dryer but into a special controlled humidity booth in a corner of the laboratory. There they dried out slowly, a process that took years in some cases. The foremast stump was so big that it had to have its own humidity chamber, a box that looked like a coffin for a giant.

Treated wooden objects from the *Defence*
lie on the Museum conservator's desk.

Many of the artifacts needed further work after they
had undergone treatment. The shoes, for example, had
fallen apart because the original thread had deteriorated.
Betty Seifert carefully stitched them up again. She also
reassembled glass bottles and ceramic pots by matching
hundreds of fragments and cementing them together.
The reassembled artifacts looked almost the way they
had when they contained galley supplies, medicine, and
liquor aboard the *Defence*.

A large, water-filled tank held all the boards of the shot
locker. Originally Dave Switzer had planned to have the
boards treated so that the shot locker could be reas-

Personnel at the Maine State Museum
glued this bottle back together.

sembled for display. But the wood had so much iron in it
from the cannonballs that preservation would have been
long, difficult, and expensive. As an alternative, Switzer
agreed on the "preservation through documentation"
approach, but with a new twist. The shot locker would

117

be documented by photographs, drawings, and a scale model. Then the boards would be redeposited in the wreck during the 1981 season.

Redeposition was also planned for some other artifacts after all the information possible had been gained from them. They were the ones not scheduled for preservation either because they could not be identified, were too large to treat easily, or were duplicates of others. The best way to keep them in fairly good condition would be to redeposit them in Stockton Harbor.

While the artifacts were undergoing treatment and documentation, they were also being cataloged under a new system. Sheli Smith, a graduate of the nautical archeology program at Texas A&M, spent a year cataloging the artifacts. A member of the *Defence* project staff in 1979, she had joined the team as a field-school student. The cataloging system divided the artifacts into "use" groups—clothing, eating, rigging, etc. Each one was photographed, and the picture of it was attached to a card on which the artifact was described.

The new cataloging system made the study of the artifacts easier. If a visitor to the Museum wanted to study pewter spoons from the *Defence*, for instance, a look at the cards would tell which drawers in the collection room held pewter spoons.

By spring, 1981, almost all the finds made through the 1979 season had been treated, documented, cataloged, and stored in the collection room. The holding tanks in the laboratory were empty and ready to receive whatever would be recovered during the 1981 season.

According to the 1981 excavation schedule that had been worked out by Dave Switzer, two areas of the hull of the *Defence* remained to be cleared—part of the stern and part of the midsection. Because there was so much to be done, eight weeks were set aside to complete the final field season. Thus, the 1981 season was longer than any of the previous ones. The workers were different too. There was to be no field school that summer, so Switzer decided to use volunteers.

During the early and final stages, most of the volunteers were old hands with previous experience at the site. One of them was Dave Switzer's daughter, Kate, a high-school student. She and her brother, Steve, had both spent summers working on the project. During the rest of the summer, most of the volunteers would be members of an organization called Earthwatch. Earthwatch is a nonprofit research organization with headquarters in Belmont, Massachusetts. Each year it advertises for volunteers to help scientists throughout the world.

On the *Defence* project, two teams of Earthwatch volunteers worked for two weeks each. They ranged in age from sixteen to sixty. Most of them were divers, but the others filled jobs on the float.

The season started in mid-June. As they arrived at the site of the wreck, the excavation team wondered what the condition of the hull would be after two years under the covering of sand and plastic sheets. On their first dive, Switzer and Smith, who served as the overall excavation supervisor in 1981, explored the wreck from bow to stern. They were relieved to find few signs of

119

Earthwatch volunteers load gear onto
the expedition boat *Grand Canyon*.

deterioration. The rest of the team, meanwhile, was put-
ting together two grids and setting them up over the stern
and midship areas. They also built a new sieve box to
replace the worn-out Priscilla. The new box was named
Pepino.

The work rhythm that had become familiar to the old
hands on the *Defence* project soon took over again.
Workers on the float hauled on ballast bucket lines while
workers on Pepino sifted through the debris brought up by
the air lift. Below, in the wreck, Earthwatch excavators
manipulated the air lift and made notes and sketches.

Workers tend the bucket lines while volunteer Kate Switzer adjusts the air lift on the floating sieve.

Marta Leskard, the on-site conservator in the early part of the season, set artifacts in tubs of water on the float.

Problems soon arose in both areas where the excavators were working. In the stern area, Warren Reiss's team uncovered a sizeable concretion that covered a large area. They had to chip at it with chisels to free it. In the midship area, Bill Bayreuther's team encountered large ballast stones that seemed to be wedged in place like a stone wall. Work progressed at a frustratingly slow speed. Switzer and Smith worried that the excavation would not be completed on time.

Bill Bayreuther gives last-minute instructions
to Earthwatch divers.

Thanks to good weather, however, no workdays were
lost and the excavation picked up speed. By the time
Peter Hentschel arrived on his first weekend visit,
enough of the stern had been uncovered to give him a
good start on his drawings.

Many of the artifacts that were coming up were similar
to those from previous years, but there were many new
ones too. Dave Switzer assembled ten small thin strips of
wood found in the midship area into a compartmented

box with a lid and a lock. Another unique find in this
area was a tall, delicate, lotus-shaped bottle of clear glass.
A bar shot, two half cannonballs connected by a bar,
turned up in the stern. Bar shot was fired from cannon
and used to destroy the rigging of enemy ships.

The large concretion in the stern had finally been pried
loose from the bottom and taken up to the float. It contained fragments of pottery, a sheet of lead, a grenade, a
number of nails, and fragments of cast iron. The cast iron
looked like the remains of a kettle. The grenade, different
in appearance from a modern grenade, was a hollow iron
ball about the size of a baseball filled with gunpowder. A

A large concretion from the stern had lead, grapeshot stools,
and ceramic fragments inside.

wooden fuse was inserted in a hole. Before the grenade was thrown at an enemy ship, it had to be lighted like a firecracker.

When the staff members were inspecting the nails and iron fragments, Heidi Miksch, the on-site conservator in the latter part of the season, noticed small bits of canvaslike fabric mixed with the metal.

"What would nails, pieces of a broken kettle, and canvas be doing in the stern?" wondered Sheli Smith.

Switzer examined the small mass of metal and canvas. "It may be langrage, a type of cannon ammunition," he said. "Langrage was scrap metal and nails packed in bags and fired at the enemy. The scraps would cut down the rigging, and the nails would cause wounds."

Heidi Miksch and Sheli Smith open a concretion.

To the best of Switzer's knowledge, the find was the first of this kind of ammunition to be recovered from a shipwreck.

The stern concretion was large, but an even larger one was uncovered in the midship area near the port side. Barrel staves and grapeshot stools were sticking out of the gray-brown mass. After the mud had been cleared from around the concretion, it was floated to the surface by means of two lift bags that were capable of moving 1,500 pounds. The huge concretion was too heavy to be

The midship concretion was towed to Sears Island by the *Grand Canyon.*

lifted up to the float, so it was tied to the stern of the expedition boat *Grand Canyon* and carried to the beach at Sears Island. At low tide, Earthwatch volunteers carefully chipped away at the mass. The staves were part of a barrel that had held 3,216 iron balls the size of large olives and plums.

Dave Switzer and Sheli Smith speculated that the crewmen dipped into the barrel to make up stands of grapeshot to replace those used during battle.

By the next to the last week of the excavation, a large section of the midship area on the port side had been cleared from the top of the frames down to the keelson. Dave Wyman dived down to look. Back on the float, he made plans to inspect the exposed structure. "Let's remove an eight-foot section of the ceiling," he said to Dave Switzer. "That will reveal enough to let me check the framing pattern."

Under Bayreuther's direction, the Earthwatch team in the midship area took off the ceiling planks one by one and piled them up beside the wreck. It was hard work. A number of saws were worn out cutting the hard oak planks. After all the planks had been removed late in the season, the old hands still at the site used an air lift to clean away the mud between the outside and inside planking.

Wyman examined the exposed frames closely. The framing pattern was similar to what he had seen in the stern. It confirmed that the *Defence* had been built by the whole mold method.

Ever since the first days of the excavation, Switzer and

Wyman had wanted to complete a photomosaic of the wreck. A photomosaic is made up of many small photographs fitted together to form one large one. The first try at a mosaic was made by Phil Voss, a field-school student, in 1978. He was fairly successful, but there were gaps in the coverage. In 1981, Rob Cole, a friend of Dave Wyman, made a second attempt. An underwater photographer for the United States Navy, Cole had experience in taking photographs in conditions of poor visibility.

Cole mounted a special attachment on his camera that

Bill Bayreuther indicates to an Earthwatch volunteer the section of grid to be excavated.

kept it at a set distance from the object being photo-graphed. A strobe light provided illumination. To take a photograph, all Cole had to do was place the attachment against the structure to be photographed and push the shutter button. No adjustment of lens for distance was necessary. The advantage of this system was that it enabled Cole to shoot many photographs during brief moments of good visibility.

Cole photographed all of the hull structure that was exposed above the mud. His work is the best photo-graphic coverage made of the sunken privateer. After Cole developed his prints, he and Wyman planned to spend many hours matching them to the outline of the wreck on the site plan. The photographs are scaled to the plan, so that any small gaps can be filled in. Eventually Switzer hopes to have a complete photomosaic of the outline of the hull.

Another job carried out in the final weeks was the re-deposition of some of the artifacts in the Museum hold-ing tanks. The staff re-examined each piece before it was taken below in case some detail had been missed. There were two redeposit sites, one in the bow and one behind the stove. Some pieces, like the boards of the shot locker, were too large to be put in with everything else, so they were simply laid in a place set aside for them.

Since the 1981 season was the last for the *Defence*, one of the goals was to leave the wreck fully protected by sandbags. While the excavation was still going on, volunteers took *Little Willy*, the outboard workboat, over to Sears Island and filled plastic bags with sand. They

128

Bags of sand and ballast were dropped onto the wreck
to cover it and leave it fully protected.

dropped these bags, as well as bags of ballast, onto the
wreck. Divers below positioned them. In the final days,
as many as sixty bags a·day went down. A total of about
600 bags were dropped in 1981.

By early August, the wreck had been completely covered with sandbags. The excavation of the *Defence* was
over. Counting the 1975 survey, six summers and well
over 2,000 hours of underwater work had been spent on
the Revolutionary War privateer.

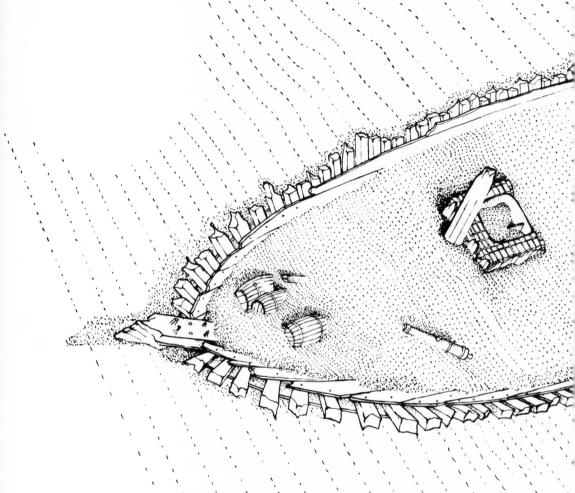

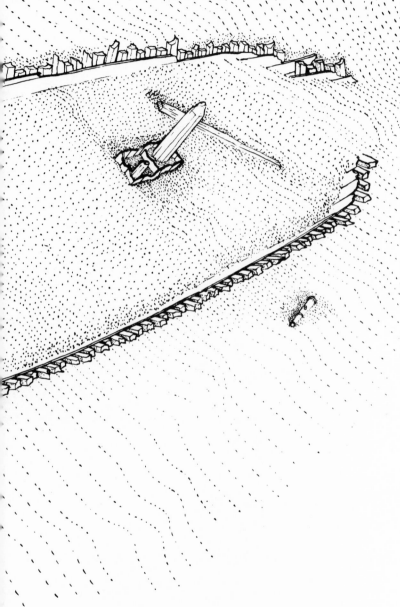

Peter Hentschel's drawing of the site as it existed
before the excavation began.

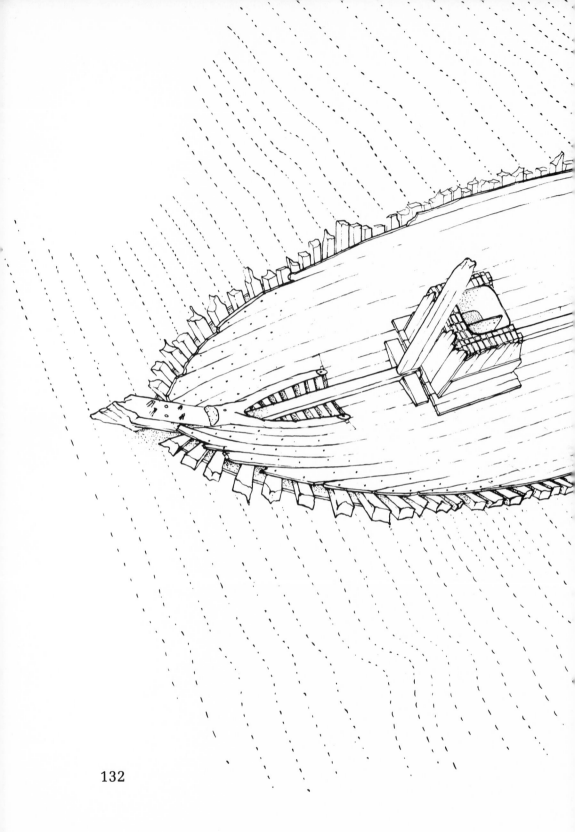

This drawing shows the exposed hull.

8

What
the *Defence*
Tells Us

During the excavation of the *Defence*, Dave Switzer and
Dave Wyman were asked one question again and again.

"Why are you spending so much time, effort, and
money excavating a ship that has no treasure?"

The *Defence* has no treasure in the usual sense. No
gold or silver was found in the wreck, not even a single
coin. But, in another sense, the Revolutionary War privateer and her artifacts are a very real treasure. When the
excavation began, the *Defence* and the *Philadelphia* were
the only two examples of American Colonial shipbuild-

135

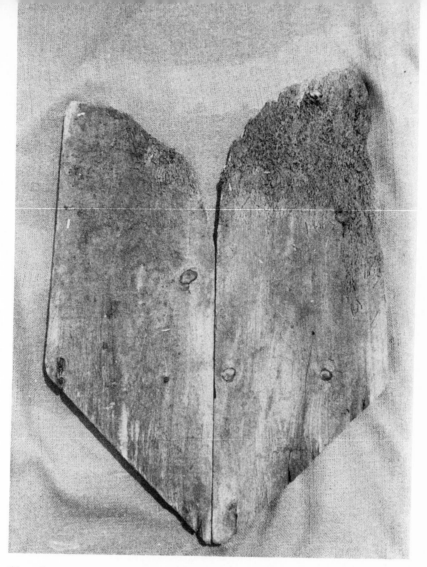

The sharp "V" formed by bow timbers indicates something about the *Defence's* shape.

ing in existence. In 1976, a Colonial vessel dating from the early 1700's was found in the Black River in South Carolina. The hull is not complete, but enough remains to indicate that its construction is different from that of the *Philadelphia* and the *Defence*. In 1981, the hull of a

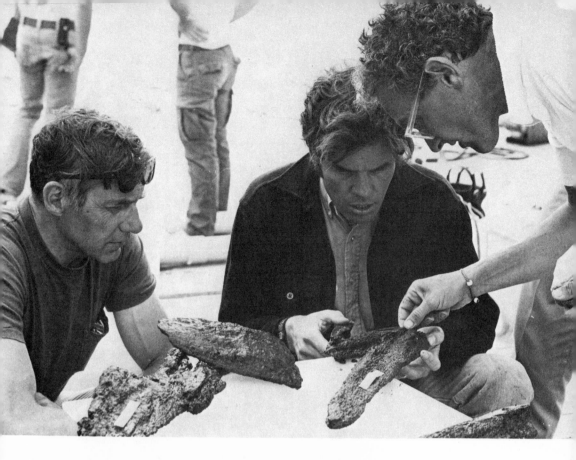

Dick Steffy, Dave Wyman, and Dave Switzer (left to right)
examine fragments of the structure.

merchant ship that also dates from the early 1700's was
found in New York City.

Of all the thousands of vessels constructed during the
Colonial period of American history, these four are the
only surviving examples.

In recent years, the wrecks of old sailing ships have
been discovered in many other areas of the world too,
including the Mediterranean, Baltic, and Caribbean Seas
and along the coasts of Great Britain, Canada, Africa, and
Australia. Up until the era of steam power, wooden sail-

ing ships were the most complicated machines built. The study of these ships and the artifacts aboard them will add immensely to present knowledge of the world's seafaring past.

The discovery and excavation of these important remains of the past also open up new opportunities in the field of nautical archeology. A number of field-school students who worked on the excavation of the *Defence* have joined George Bass and other nautical archeologists as they probe seabeds throughout the world in search of shipwrecks. Now that more scuba divers understand the importance of shipwrecks, there is a good chance that they will be left undisturbed, like the *Defence*.

The interpretation of the *Defence* will continue for many years after the excavation. As they examine the artifacts, plans, and other documentation, Dave Switzer, Dave Wyman, and Sheli Smith have begun to create a picture of life aboard the privateer. They are also learning more about what kind of ship she was and what happened to her after she sank.

The three investigators already have learned much about the ship that sailed with the Penobscot Expedition. To begin with, she must have been a very crowded ship. Historical records tell us that there were 100 men aboard, but the midship area, where the crew hung their hammocks and stored their sea chests, is only about twenty-five feet by twenty feet. Furthermore, the distance between the top of the ballast and the underside of the deck is scarcely more than six feet.

Tall crewmen must have been particularly uncomfort-

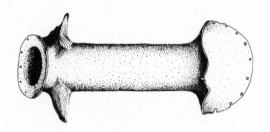

Scuppers used to drain water off the deck provide clues
to the width of the bulwark, the side of the vessel above the deck.

able below deck. Judging from the small size of their
shoes, however, few of the crewmen were tall.

The crew's quarters in midship must have been the
busiest area, but the next busiest was certainly around
the cookstove. Artifacts indicate the crew's messhall was
there, and certain crewmen like the bos'un, carpenter,
and gunner all had cubbies there to store supplies. The
galley may also have been the dispensary for medical
supplies, since the medicine bottles were found near
there. Probably no physician was aboard, so the cook or
bos'un may have been responsible for giving out the
medicine.

The primary food-storage area was undoubtedly in the
bow, where many barrels were found. But barrel staves
and the barrel top with the name of the contents—*Pork
32 Pieces Ea Ford*—were also found near the shot locker

in the midship area. Since the officers' quarters were nearby in the stern, this barrel might have held a better grade of salt pork destined for use in the officers' mess.

Reconstructing the pattern of life in the stern is harder than in other areas, because the stern was severely damaged. Traditionally, the officers of a Colonial vessel would have their quarters in a cabin just above the magazine in the stern. The magazine was almost certainly in

The location of this barrel indicates that the pork in it may have been meant for the officers' mess.

the stern, judging from the damage found in that area. Nothing remains of a cabin, but the few artifacts found do suggest that the men who used them had more means than ordinary seamen.

Dave Wyman is using the plans and other information he collected on the structure of the *Defence* to get some idea of what kind of ship she was. One thing plans can show, for instance, is whether a vessel is fast or slow. The three-dimensional plan of the *Defence* made from the measurements Wyman and Hentschel took shows the ship had a V-shaped hull, which suggests a fast sailer.

Comparing the profile plan with those for American-built vessels of the period, Wyman noticed a similarity

This piece of leather was a book cover.

between the *Defence* and ships built in the Chesapeake Bay area of Virginia. Both have V-shaped hulls and sharp bows. According to the late Howard Chapelle, an authority on old American sailing ships, these Virginia-built vessels were fast and features of their design "migrated" to Massachusetts during the Revolutionary War. There is a strong possibility, Wyman believes, that the *Defence* may have been one of the earliest examples of this type of fast-sailing vessel in the northern United States.

Did the design of the *Defence* migrate from Virginia to

A flat plan of the bow.

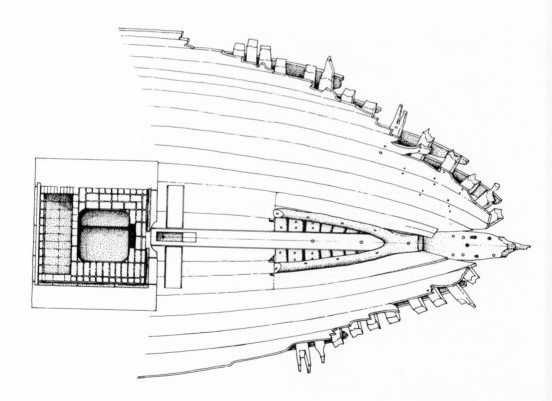

PLAN - FOREMAST TO STEM

Massachusetts? Only further research and perhaps a little luck will provide the answer. There are other unanswered questions about the structure of the privateer too. One of the most puzzling concerns the way she was built. Why are there so many signs of hasty workmanship? In many respects, the *Defence* was a well-built vessel. She was constructed of good materials, and some parts of her structure show signs of careful craftsmanship.

The keelson, for example, was carefully shaped, and the cookstove was an unusually solid structure. In fact, the cookstove and shot locker hardly seem to have come from the same ship.

Perhaps the uneven shot locker was a last-minute addition. But the hasty workmanship in the framing is harder to understand. One explanation may lie in the commercial character of privateers. They were underwritten by private citizens who looked on them as an investment. As such, they may have been built to provide a quick return, not to give long service. Since no other privateers are known from the Colonial era, no one knows whether the *Defence* is typical of this type of ship or not.

The artifacts aboard the *Defence* not only tell something of life aboard the vessel, they show what happened to her after she sank. In 1976, Cynthia Orr made a drawing of the position of every artifact in the trench that had been dug through the stove area. When Switzer and Wyman studied the drawing later, they saw that the heavier artifacts rested above the lighter ones. Ship's knees and deck planking, for instance, lay above shoes, plates, and other small objects.

Dave Switzer believes that the relationship of the artifacts gives some clues as to what happened to the *Defence* as she lay in the seabed. His theory is that when the *Defence* sank, much of her deck was intact, although it was probably damaged by fire. A mast may well have stuck up above the surface for many years. Gradually the weight of the hull and its tons of ballast caused the hull to sink deeper and deeper into the mud. Meanwhile, the light leather and wood artifacts that were floating within the hull had become waterlogged. They sank to the

Cynthia Orr's drawing shows the contents of the stove trench. Notice that the hull has a sharp, rather than a "U"-shaped, bottom.

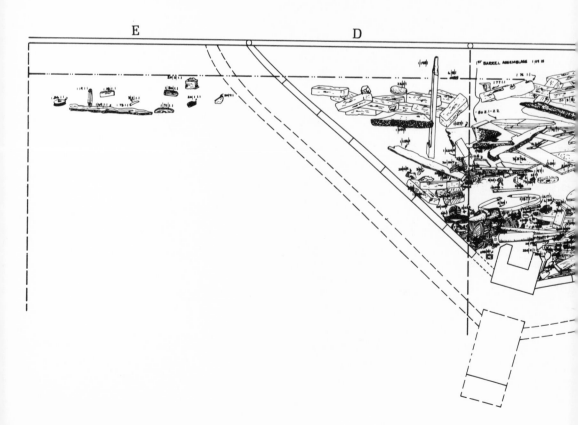

ballast or to the bottom of the hull, where the metal artifacts already lay.

The deck, which never acquired a protective coating of mud, deteriorated as the years passed. Mud and silt filtered through holes in the deck and buried the artifacts below. Finally the deck gave way, and the planks and other timbers that remained fell on top of the artifacts and were soon buried too. The deck may not have collapsed until this century. In *The History of Stockton Springs,* Alice Ellis describes seeing a ship with its deck still intact below the waters of Stockton Harbor when she was a girl.

Archeological work on land or underwater is often frustrating, because the artifacts cannot tell a complete

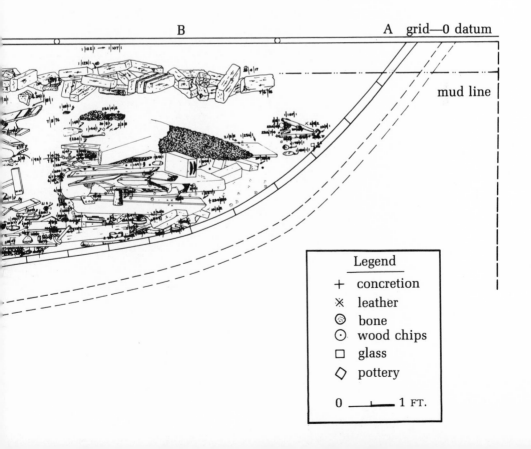

In his Plymouth State College office,
Dave Switzer studies the plan of the hull structure.

story. Extensive research is usually necessary to make
them yield even a few facts. But even if the *Defence* and
the artifacts taken from her hull tell only part of their
story, they make present-day knowledge of the history of
Colonial ships and the men who sailed them a little more
complete.

146

Defence
Excavation
Personnel

PERMANENT STAFF MEMBERS
Dr. David C. Switzer, Director
David B. Wyman, Associate Director
Peter Hentschel, Structure Artist
Stephen Brooke, Maine State Museum Conservator

STAFF MEMBERS
Dr. George Bass (1975)
William Bayreuther, Trench Team Leader (1981)
Quentin Blaine, Staff Excavator (1979),
   Assistant Team Leader (1981)

Jonathan Blumenfeld, Trench Team Leader (1977, 1978)
Robert Cole, Photographer (1981)
Grant Hackett, Recorder (1979)
Faith Harrington, Finds Artist (1978)
Faith Hentschel, Excavation Supervisor (1975)
Helen Hillhouse, Finds Artist (1977)
Paul Hundley, Dive Master (1978)
Shelley Lang, Excavator (1979)
Marta Leskard, Conservator (1981)
Heidi Miksch, Conservator (1981)
Kenneth Morris, Conservator (1977)
Martha Oatway, Conservation Assistant (1978)
Cynthia Orr, Student Staff Assistant (1976),
    Trench Team Leader (1977)
Nancy Orton, Trench Team Leader (1978)
Paula Perlman, Excavator (1979)
Shelley Reisman, Conservation Technician (1976)
Warren Reiss, Dive Master (1976, 1977),
    Assistant Photographer (1976, 1977),
    Structure Recorder (1978), Trench Team Leader (1981)
Steven Ross, Excavator (1979)
Elizabeth Seifert,
    Museum Conservation Technician (1977)
Matthew Sizemore, Excavator (1979)
Roger Smith, Photographer (1978)
Sheli Smith, Excavator (1979),
    Assistant Director (1981)
Allen Spencer, Excavator (1979)
Richard Steffy, INA Ship Reconstructor
    (1976, 1977, 1978)

Avery Stone, Recorder (1977, 1978)

Mary Strouse, Excavation Supervisor-Recorder (1975)

Richard Swete, Structure Recorder (1978),
    Dive Master (1981)

Rhys Townsend, Student Staff Assistant (1976)

Philip Voss, Photographer (1976, 1977)

FIELD-SCHOOL STUDENTS

Daniel Bartley

David Bell

Michael Biel

Thomas Birchett

Quentin Blaine

Jonathan Blumenfeld

Elizabeth Brandt

Paul Burke

Carolyn Carter

Donald Charland

Andrew Chase

Thomas Darlington

James Durana

Wendy Feuer

Richard Geffken

Henry Graham

Richard Green

Helen Hillhouse

Paul Hundley

Paul Johnston

William Justiss

Daniel Koski-Karell

Shelley Lang

Marta Leskard

Samuel Margolin

Sheila Matthews

Carol Olsen

Cynthia Orr

Nancy Orton

Glenn Pennoyer

Paula Perlman

Sr. Mary John Philip, BVM

Kenneth Pott

Steven Ross

Joseph Schwarzer II

Matthew Sizemore

Roger Smith

Sheli Smith

Allen Spencer

Barbara Stucki

Marilyn Staehle

Richard Swete

Allyn Taylor

Rhys Townsend

VOLUNTEERS
Jonathan Blumenfeld (1981)
William Doll
Katharine Switzer
Stephen Switzer
Jonathan Wyman

EARTHWATCH VOLUNTEERS

Team 1	Team 2
Gavin Ames	Leroy and Julia Clapp
Jamie Brickle	Margaret Cowin
Jane Coddington	Catherine Diekmann
Margaret Cowin	Charles Eilber
Joseph Cozzi	Fiske and Nancy Field
John and Elise Frater	Theodore Harrison
Rosemunde Hammond	Kevin Harrison
Allan McClelland	Larry Jones
David Phol	Stanley and Kevin Kelley
Eric Raymond	Jackson Kendall
Joseph Solomon	Martha Radke
Paul Switzer	
Kent Walker	
Frank Winter	

Index

151

cannon, 32, 33, 37, 38, 38*, 40,
42-45, 44*, 45*, 67, 67*, 81,
123
cannonballs, 33, 34, 34*, 55,
81, 123
Castine (Maine), 28, 31, 37, 48,
75, 89, 100
cataloging of artifacts, 61*,
61-62, 63*, 118
ceramic ware, 42, 70, 88, 89*,
92, 116
Chapelle, Howard, 142
Chesapeake Bay (Va.), 142
Cole, Rob, 127-28
Collier, Sir George, 16, 24, 29
Collins, Captain, 24
conservation of artifacts, 51,
58, 75, 89*, 89-93, 92*, 95,
97, 105
Constitution, 97
    supports landing on
        Nautilus Island, 18
    wreck located in Stockton
        Harbor, 29-32
cookstove, 42, 43*, 66, 73-75,
143

Davis quadrant, 88, 88*
deck, 57, 101, 106*, 145
Defence (see also specific
    listings)
    artifact conservation,
        89-93, 115-18
    artifact recovery plan,
        59-62
    cannons recovered, 37-40,
        42
    enters Stockton Harbor,
        23-24

excavation by Maine
    Maritime Academy
    students, 41-46
explodes and sinks, 24
first artifacts recovered,
    32-36
hull found, 36-37
importance of, 135-37
interpretation of, 138-46
measurement of hull,
    96-112
1975 INA survey, 51-58
1976 excavation season,
    60-77
1977-1979 excavation
    seasons, 79-89, 98-112
1981 excavation season,
    115-29
sails west after leaving
    Bagaduce, 21, 23
sails with Penobscot
    Expedition, 15

Earthwatch, 119, 120, 122*,
126
Edgerton, Harold, 30
Edmonds, John, 15, 24
Ellis, Alice, 145

fid, 67
field school (INA), 47, 48, 58,
80, 138
food, 42, 66, 69, 73
Fort George (Maine), 18, 19*,
20, 28, 28*
frames, 101, 105, 107, 108,
126, 143
freeze-dryer, 92, 92*, 115
futtocks, 101

152

privateer, 15, 143

rammer, 67, 67*
redeposition of artifacts, 118,
 128
Reisman, Shelley, 75
Reiss, Warren, 121
Revere, Paul, 16, 17*, 18, 20,
 25
ribbon, 69, 69*
rigging, 34
Russell Hart Nautical Museum,
 110

sailmaker's palm, 67
Saltonstall, Dudley, 16, 19, 20
scuppers, 34, 139*
sea chest, 89
Sea Grant program, 30
Searle, William F., 31, 41, 42,
 46, 47, 48
Sears Island (Maine), 29, 31*,
 32, 126, 128
Seifert, Betty, 63*, 95
shirt, 69
shoes, 54, 67, 68*, 85, 88, 116
shot locker, 81, 83*, 84*,
 84-85, 116-17, 128, 139, 143
Smith, Sheli, 118, 119, 121,
 124, 124*, 126, 138
Smithsonian Institution, 45, 47
Snow, Lin, 106*
sonar, 30-31
Steffy, Richard, 100, 137*

stern, 54, 62, 88-89, 108, 121,
 123, 125, 140-41
Stockton Harbor (Maine), 23,
 23*, 24, 29, 30, 31, 32, 51,
 57, 118, 145
Switzer, David C., 47-48, 49*,
 51, 53, 54, 55, 57, 58, 59, 62,
 63*, 66, 70, 71, 73, 75, 79,
 80*, 81, 84, 85, 88, 89, 93,
 95, 96, 96*, 98, 101, 102*,
 103, 108, 110, 117, 119, 121,
 122, 124-25, 126, 135, 138,
 143-44, 146*
Switzer, Kate, 119, 121*
Switzer, Steve, 119

tankards, wooden, 85
Texas A&M University, 80, 118
tompion, 81
Townsend, Rhys, 75, 102*,
 102-3
trunnels, 101, 108

Voss, Phil, 127

Warren, 15, 18, 22, 23, 27-28
Wasa, 96, 97
Wyman, David B., 31, 32, 37,
 38, 42, 46, 48, 50*, 54, 55,
 57, 58, 59, 75, 81, 93, 96, 98,
 99*, 100, 101, 102, 102*,
 105, 106*, 108, 109, 109*,
 110-11, 112, 126, 127, 128,
 135, 138, 141-42, 143

About the Authors

Barbara Ford was born in St. Louis and received her B.S. from St. Louis University and her M.A. from New York University. Before becoming a full-time writer, she was senior editor for *Science Digest*. She has won awards for her science reporting, and five of her books have been named "Outstanding Science Books for Children" in their respective years by the National Science Teachers Association. Ms. Ford presently lives in New Jersey with her husband.

David C. Switzer was born in Portland, Maine. He received a B.A. degree from the University of Maine and M.A. and Ph.D. degrees from the University of Connecticut. A professor of history at Plymouth State College, he has been involved in marine archeology since 1974, working as an expedition member or the director of various underwater archeological projects. He currently lives with his family in Plymouth, New Hampshire.